UNHIDE & SEEK

*Live Your Best Life
Do Your Best Work*

ALSO BY
Ruth Rathblott, MSW

Singlehandedly

Learning to Unhide and Embrace Connection

Advanced Praise for **Unhide & Seek**

Unhide & Seek is an invaluable resource for leaders and individuals striving to foster inclusivity, authenticity, and empathy in their personal and professional lives. Ruth Rathblott illuminates how hiding is a problem that can hinder our potential and provides a compelling roadmap to unhiding as the solution. This book is a must-read for anyone committed to personal growth and organizational success.

—**Roger W. Ferguson, Jr.,** Immediate Past President & CEO, TIAA

Ruth Rathblott's *Unhide & Seek* is a powerful call to action for women and men alike. Women are often told they're "too this" or "too that," which fuels their need to hide parts of themselves to fit into professional environments. Ruth's empathetic approach and practical steps show how unhiding and being our authentic selves can create more diverse and inclusive organizational cultures where individuals from all walks of life can succeed. This book is an essential guide for anyone committed to fostering spaces where everyone feels they belong and can thrive.

—**Shelley Zalis,** Founder and CEO of The Female Quotient

Unhide & Seek is a transformative read that emphasizes the importance of transparency and authenticity. Ruth's insights on courage and community offer a compelling vision for creating inclusive environments where everyone can feel valued and connected. Unhiding not only fosters a sense of belonging but also brings the freedom to be one's true self.

—**Jessica Sibley,** Chief Executive Officer, TIME

Ruth's book is an important guide for leaders who want to foster innovation and engagement. *Unhide & Seek* shows how engaged leaders build strong teams and create cultures of belonging and support. Ruth emphasizes that leaders must go first in demonstrating vulnerability and setting the tone for openness. This book is essential for anyone committed to leading with integrity and inspiring others.

—**Steve Odland,** President and CEO of The Conference Board

Unhide & Seek reveals how hiding holds us back and provides a practical framework for unhiding. It empowers readers to build deeper, more meaningful connections with themselves and others, and experience the freedom that comes with embracing their true selves.

—**Dorie Clark,** Wall Street Journal bestselling author
of *The Long Game* and executive education faculty,
Columbia Business School

Ruth's first book *Singlehandedly* helped us understand the pervasiveness of hiding. *Unhide and Seek* goes further by helping to release the burden of hiding, allowing us to create space for ourselves and others to operate unapologetically and feel connected while doing it. Ruth's emphasis on humanity and empathy creates a roadmap that helps build safe spaces and connections, making it a must-read for anyone committed to fostering inclusion and belonging in their personal and professional lives.

—**Rocki Howard,** Founder, Diversiology.io

So many of us have felt the need to hide parts of ourselves—it can lead to feeling disconnected. When we unhide, we ignite inclusion and belonging. This book is a transformative tool for creating environments where disabilities and all differences are celebrated, allowing everyone to feel seen, heard, and empowered to thrive

—**Meg O'Connell,** Founder and CEO of Global Disability Inclusion

Unhide & Seek is indispensable for those committed to fostering equity and belonging. Ruth's profound insights and practical strategies propose 'unhiding' as a transformative approach to cultivating inclusive environments where people can feel seen, valued, and empowered to embrace their authentic selves. This book is a call to action for leaders at every level.

—**Darren Walker,** President of the Ford Foundation

Freedom. Focus. Fulfillment.

UNHIDE & SEEK

Live Your Best Life
Do Your Best Work

RUTH RATHBLOTT, MSW

RuthRathblott.com

Produced by Singlehanded Press

ISBN 979-8-9863847-4-0 (Paperback)
ISBN 979-8-9863847-5-7 (E-book)
ISBN 979-8-9863847-6-4 (Audiobook)

For bulk purchase, book clubs, and booking, contact:

Ruth Rathblott, MSW
ruth@ruthrathblott.com
ruthrathblott.com

Because of the dynamic nature of the Internet, web address or links contained in this book may change after publication.

The author of this book does not dispense medical advice, or prescribe the use of any technique as a form of treatment for physical, emotional, or medical problems without the advice of a physician, either directly or indirectly. The intent of the author is only to offer information of a general nature to help you and your quest for emotional, physical, and spiritual well-being , in the event, you use any of the information in this book for yourself the author and the publisher assumed no responsibility for your actions.

This is a work of nonfiction. However, the identities of certain individuals have been changed to protect their privacy.

Library of Congress Control Number: 2024915018

Cover Design: Alexander Valchev

Edited by Elizabeth Arterberry and Christine Borris

Interior design by AuthorSupport.com, Interior Graphics: Martin Veleski

FIRST EDITION

For all who seek to unhide and embrace their best selves—
you are not alone.

I have experienced incredible freedom through unhiding,
and I encourage you to embrace this journey and enjoy its
profound benefits.

I look forward to meeting you on this path of unhiding
and seeking.

Table of Contents

Welcome to Unhide & Seek

This book will guide you through a transformative journey of self-discovery and authenticity. By the end of this book, you will have the tools and insights needed to unhide your best self, fostering deeper connections and a more fulfilling life both personally and professionally.

WHY THIS BOOK?

Have you ever felt the need to hide a part of yourself to fit in? That moment, you tuck just a tiny part of yourself away to have it go unnoticed.

Most of us have. Maybe even all of us.

You may not realize it, but every day, you make choices—some conscious, others less so—about what parts of yourself to reveal and what to conceal. Whether driven by fear, a desire for acceptance, or the need to protect your vulnerabilities, these decisions shape your relationships, career, and inner sense of freedom.

Maybe you hide your mental health struggles out of fear of stigma; conceal your socioeconomic status to avoid judgment; keep your religious beliefs private to prevent discrimination; or mask your ADHD symptoms to fit in at work. Others in your life might hide aspects of their identity, such as their sexual orientation or gender identity, their efforts to recover from addiction, a chronic illness, or even life goals they struggle to reach. These choices to hide are often rooted in a desire for safety and belonging, and can significantly impact how you navigate your personal and professional life.

Hiding is a pervasive problem that stifles creativity and innovation, drains energy, and prevents genuine connections; it creates performance problems in *every* aspect of our lives.

Drawing from psychological theories, such as Carl G. Jung's *archetypes* and Abraham Maslow's *hierarchy of needs,* I decided to investigate how these fascinating ideas might further illuminate the phenomena of hiding and unhiding. Jung's archetypes can help us understand the different personas we adopt to protect ourselves. Maslow's hierarchy of needs shows us how hiding impacts our ability to meet our fundamental needs and achieve our highest level, self-actualization. These theories provide us with a deeper understanding of why we hide and offer valuable insights into how we can begin to unhide.

Over the past few years, through my research, writing, and professional speaking, I've engaged with global audiences on the topic of hiding. These conversations have led to powerful moments where individuals share their pain, their experiences of hiding, and the relief that comes with unhiding. From this work, I have identified three key insights: 1) It is universal—most of us are hiding. 2) It is lonely; most of us think we are the only ones hiding. 3) It is exhausting—hiding takes a toll on our mental and physical health, leaving us to feel isolated and disconnected.

In my first book, *Singlehandedly: Learning to Unhide and Embrace Connection*, I shared my twenty-five-year journey of hiding my limb difference, a partially formed left hand known as amniotic band syndrome. The memoir details my struggles with self-acceptance and societal pressures and how I found joy and freedom in unhiding. By sharing stories and insights, I encouraged readers to embrace their differences and build connection. *Singlehandedly* also broadens the conversation on diversity and inclusion, encompassing the experiences of those with apparent and non-apparent disabilities. It highlights the power of vulnerability, the importance of community, and the transformative impact of unhiding.

While that story was my personal journey, *this* book, *Unhide & Seek,* shifts the spotlight to <u>you</u>. It delves into the universal experience of hiding, the ways you hide and unhide, and the tools for transformation to assist in developing your curiosity and introspection. The stories come from various sources: people I've met after speaking engagements and my TEDx talk; outreach with readers of my first book; and research data that I've collected on what people choose to hide.

Unhide & Seek weaves psychological insights into a narrative, making it more than just an educational resource—it's a call to action. It invites you to engage in lifelong learning focused on self-awareness and understanding others' paths. It asks the following questions:

1. What are you hiding, and how is it holding you back from thriving and connecting?
2. What happens when you stop hiding?
3. What if you embraced your best self and shattered the confines of conformity?

This journey of unhiding is not just about revealing our differences—it's about celebrating them and finding the freedom to live authentically. It's time to step out of the shadows and into the light, to unhide and thrive!

By acknowledging the hidden parts of yourself, you unlock the power that comes from truly seeing and being seen. You open up opportunities for authentic relationships, personal growth, and a more inclusive and empathetic world. Unhiding is a path to freedom, self-acceptance, and deeper connections with others. Welcome to the journey of discovering and embracing your best self.

Welcome to UNHIDE & SEEK!

How to Use This Book

Whether you're new to these ideas on hiding and unhiding or are familiar with them from previous work, this book expands on them in fresh, engaging ways. You can start here for an overview or read *Singlehandedly* first to understand how these concepts played out in my life. Either way, I hope that you'll find enriching insights and practical strategies.

Unhide & Seek is designed to be worked through, not just read through. Imagine yourself as the hero/heroine of this story, embarking on a quest to discover and embrace your best self. Every hero/heroine's journey begins with a challenge—a moment when you recognize the need for change. In this context, it's the realization that hiding parts of yourself—due to fear, shame, or societal pressure—is holding you back from thriving.

Answering that call means stepping into the unknown and leaving behind what feels safe. This book will guide you through this transition, helping you identify and acknowledge your hidden aspects and understand the reasons behind these choices. By taking this step, you engage in self-discovery and transformation.

Every hero/heroine faces trials along their journey. In *Unhide & Seek*, these challenges include confronting fears, embracing vulnerability, and managing relation-ships. Each chapter provides tools and strategies to over-come these obstacles, illustrated through practical exer-cises and personal stories.

As you progress, you will continue to discover and unhide parts of yourself, experiencing the empowerment that comes with authenticity. By embracing your unique identity, you unlock new levels of creativity, innovation, and connection in all areas of your life.

The final stage in the hero/heroine's journey is the return with the treasure—the wisdom and knowledge gained. As you conclude *Unhide & Seek*, you will carry with you the treasure of self-acceptance and authenticity. This newfound freedom will enrich your life and inspire those around you to embark on their own journeys. You will have a community to connect with, ensuring that you are not alone.

Understanding why you hide and recognizing its cost is crucial for connection and self-actualization. This involves more than identifying hidden aspects; it's about creating a life where you can freely express your best self and enjoy your uniqueness.

You will explore strategies to break down the barriers of fear, shame, and societal expectations that compel us to hide. This book is about understanding the toll hiding takes and setting the stage for a journey toward openness and authenticity—it's about unhiding.

I've seen firsthand the transformative power of environments where everyone can be their fullest self, as well as the challenges and missed opportunities when individuals feel they must conceal their identities. Creating psychological safety is crucial in these healthy environments. When people feel safe to be open and authentic, it not only enhances their personal growth but also boosts team collaboration, innovation, and overall performance.

While the archetypes and strategies provided offer a framework for action, remember that your journey is unique and shaped by personal history, culture, and circumstances. Different cultures have expectations, norms, and pressures that shape our tendencies to hide certain aspects of our identity. Use the insights here as starting points, and feel free to adapt them to your life. It may be helpful to seek additional resources like professional counseling, tailored workshops, or online support groups focused on personal growth, mental health, and diversity issues for further guidance.

Learning to unhide is a continuum, where you may move back and forth as you navigate different experiences. It's important to approach each step with self-compassion, focusing on the movement toward greater self-acceptance. Wherever you find yourself on the continuum is exactly where you need to be right now.

Hiding <————————————> Unhiding

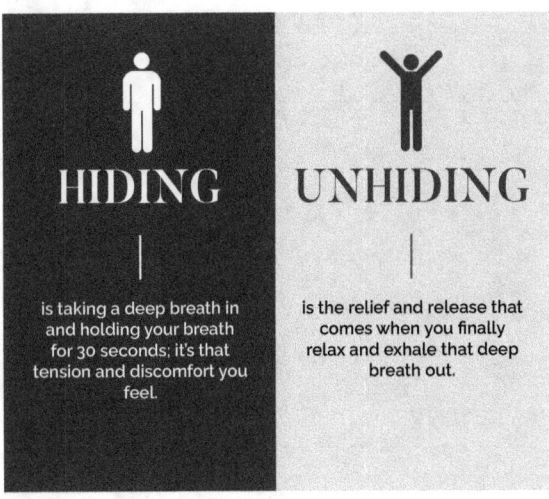

Try this exercise.

Take a deep breath in. Hold it for 30 seconds. Release with a deep exhale.

Hiding is like holding a deep breath, creating tension and discomfort, while unhiding is the relief and release you feel when you finally exhale, finding balance and ease.

NOTES

PART ONE

Hiding

In the first section, we delve into the concept of hiding. You'll learn about how we conceal parts of ourselves and the psychological and societal pressures that drive these behaviors. This section sets the foundation by defining what it means to hide and why it is such a pervasive issue.

HIDING DEFINED

In my first book, *Singlehandedly*, I defined "hiding" as follows:

- Turning inward and deliberately not sharing a part of yourself for fear of judgment, criticism, rejection, or assumptions based on stigmas and stereotypes.
- Feeling shame and loneliness; lacking a connection to yourself and others.
- Affecting how you show up and act because you feel unsafe.

Synonyms: *covering, lying, masking, passing, concealing.*

Since then, I have deepened my understanding of hiding and added the following to the definition:

- Hiding impacts many aspects of our lives, though its effects may not always be apparent. We might stay in relationships that should've ended, avoid personal growth by busying ourselves with tasks, or conceal our opinions to remain comfortable. We may hide behind beliefs without examining them, or behind our children's successes rather than pursuing our own goals. We even hide behind power and titles, making it harder to connect with others and build trust.

- Hiding prevents us from forming real connections and impacts our performance. We may choose to focus on drama and appearances to avoid the hard work of self-acceptance and genuine connection. Hiding offers excuses to avoid building relationships and making progress.

- Hiding causes us to constantly question how much of ourselves to reveal, whether at work, spending time with friends, or alone. This endless self-monitoring can be exhausting and may limit our true potential and creativity. Hiding can make us feel isolated and drained, affecting our mental and physical health. It creates gaps in our experiences and weakens the connections that are crucial for a fulfilling life.

- Hiding part of ourselves can start as a deliberate and strategic act, but over time, it can become second nature or involuntary; we may not even realize that we are hiding. What begins as a conscious decision to protect oneself can evolve into automatic behavior, making it even harder to break free and unhide.

Continuous hiding chips away at our self-confidence and ability to connect with others. We are not always the most reliable narrators of our own stories, as our views can be blurred by fears, insecurities, and external messages. Recognizing how we hide is the first step toward change. By identifying and acknowledging these behaviors, we can start to move toward living a more authentic and fulfilling life—we can find freedom.

CHAPTER 1

Why We Hide

Discover why you hide parts of yourself. This chapter will help you understand the fear, shame, and societal pressure that make you keep certain things about yourself a secret. By recognizing these factors, you'll start your journey toward a more open and true-to-yourself life, understanding the universal nature of hiding and its emotional toll.

When was the first time you noticed you were different? Or felt you had to hide part of yourself to fit in? Perhaps you held back the correct answer or remained silent when you had a valuable idea. Maybe you altered how you looked, spoke, or acted to blend in. Most of us have—at some point in our lives—adapted ourselves to avoid standing out.

For me, the moment of feeling different came at age thirteen, when I boarded a yellow school bus to a new school. Someone noticed me and stared at my small left hand for a little too long, making me really uncomfortable. My face flushed with embarrassment. I knew I didn't want anyone else to see it and stare. My immediate impulse was to hide it—to tuck my little hand in my pocket, so that I could be seen like everyone else, as a person with two "normal" hands. By hiding my little hand, I believed I could blend in and avoid unwanted attention; no one had to know.

Like most teens who already feel self-conscious, having a visible difference made my anxiety worse. Hiding became a habit for me, a way to protect myself and avoid uncomfortable situations. It also seemed to make others more comfortable, allowing them to ignore my difference and sparing us both their reaction. I lived in hiding for twenty-five years. Hiding shaped every decision I made, consciously and unconsciously; it became a coping strategy. I thought it protected me. I thought I was alone in my hiding and no one would understand. I was wrong.

I had to learn how to unhide.

Since I began unhiding and sharing how I hid my difference, I have encountered many others with similar stories of hiding, those who have felt the need to cover part of themselves to fit in. For instance, a woman who covered her burn scars with makeup and creative hairstyles because she felt the scars ruined her appearance, and a man who avoided speaking up in meetings because of his stutter. I also heard from a woman now in her forties who hid a childhood illness until it became too serious to conceal, and another woman who kept an abusive relationship hidden from friends and family. Additionally, a man working in technology concealed his age for fear of being seen as old, and a person who hid their ADHD and anxiety, thinking people wouldn't accept them. The stories are endless.

People hide many aspects of themselves, both visible and invisible. These range from physical disabilities and mental health issues—like depression, bipolar disorder, addiction, and anxiety—to neurodiversity (ADHD, autism, dyslexia) to beyond disability, people hide their age, educational background, financial situation, relationship status, religion, and more. Most of us want to fit in and feel safe; we often think we are the only ones hiding something.

HIDDEN VOICES: UNVEILING
PERSONAL STRUGGLES

These powerful testimonies of hiding provide a glimpse into
the many hidden struggles shared with me during my talks
at various organizations and through emails. These stories
reveal a broad range of personal and professional challenges
that often go unspoken. As you read through them, reflect
on what *you* keep hidden and its impact on your life.

I hide...

- My anxiety. My depression.
- My recovery from alcoholism.
- The extreme stress I face juggling issues with a sick
  family member, kids, work, personal care, etc.
- Future aspirations in the company.
- My wealth.
- My limited finances: I'm deeply stressed, living
  paycheck to paycheck.
- How in debt I am.
- That it takes me a little longer than some to
  process information.
- My family background.
- That I am an extremely creative person who tends
  to squash those tendencies at work.

- Vulnerabilities: It's easier to say I'm fine than to say something bothers me.
- My attention-deficit/hyperactivity disorder (ADHD) symptoms and that I really filter my conversations/behaviors in the workplace. I often strive for a level of perfectionism that isn't realistic in an attempt to hide any shortcomings.
- My education.
- That I'm divorced.
- My lack of education.
- My weight.
- I don't speak for fear of being judged, reprimanded, or put in my place. It comes from having been treated that way by people, especially when I was young.
- My religion.
- I suffer with self-confidence, but I never share that with anyone.
- My "blackness," when it "makes sense." I hide my "whiteness," when it "makes sense." I hide my sexuality. I hide my body.
- I like girls, and my parents think I will marry a nice boy and give them grandkids.
- My childhood trauma.
- A suicide attempt.

- That my partner has anxiety and depression.
- Being a transgender woman, for safety.
- My limb difference.
- That I have children.
- That I have a child with mental health challenges.
- My cancer diagnosis.
- That I smoke.
- My disability.
- That I'm divorced.
- That I am deaf in one ear. I have gotten so used to hiding it that sometimes I forget.
- How lonely I feel, and how much I struggle with making connections.

The list goes on.

Whether concealing mental health struggles, cultural identity, or personal challenges, the common thread is a fear of rejection and judgment. Maintaining these façades is exhausting and prompts us to question why we feel the need to hide. The answer often comes from external messages about what's "normal" and how we should fit in, combined with internal narratives about acceptance and rejection.

Embracing our hidden voices and bringing them to light is the first step toward true freedom and connection.

This act allows us to break down barriers, challenge stigmas, and create environments where authenticity is celebrated. By doing so, we pave the way for a more compassionate and understanding world where everyone has the opportunity to unhide, thrive, and belong.

HIDING INVENTORY: WHAT ARE YOU HIDING?

Now that you have a fuller definition of hiding and have read about some ways others have hidden, let's tune into you. The inventory on the next page is an opportunity to reflect on your personal life experiences and identify what you might be hiding. Understanding these hidden aspects of yourself can be the first step toward unhiding and embracing your true self. First, let's look at common ways in which people might hide.

- **Mental Health**: Many people hide their anxiety, depression, or other mental health conditions due to fear of stigma or judgment. For instance, to avoid being seen as weak or 'unfit,' you might pretend everything is fine at home or in the workplace, even when you're struggling internally.
- **Socioeconomic Status**: You might conceal your financial struggles to fit in with peers who appear

more affluent, not sharing worries about money or pretending to afford activities that stretch your budget. Alternatively, you may hide your wealth to avoid standing out.

- **Physical Health Issues**: Some hide chronic illnesses or disabilities to avoid judgment or discrimination. For example, you might downplay the severity of a health condition at work to avoid being seen as less capable.

- **Sexual Orientation or Gender Identity**: Fear of rejection or discrimination might lead you to hide your sexual orientation or gender identity. This could mean using gender-neutral language about a partner or avoiding conversations about your personal life.

- **Religious Beliefs**: You may hide your religious beliefs to avoid conflict or prejudice. This can include not discussing your faith practices or downplaying their importance when you're in social or professional settings.

- **Personal Aspirations and Dreams**: Sometimes, people hide their true aspirations because they fear ridicule or believe their dreams are unrealistic. This could take the form of not sharing your ambition to change careers or pursue a creative passion.

- **Family Background**: You might conceal aspects of your family background, such as a history of addiction or incarceration, to avoid judgment and maintain a certain image people have of you.
- **Relationship Issues**: It's not uncommon to hide problems in personal relationships to maintain a façade of perfection. For example, you might pretend everything is perfect in your marriage or partnership, even when facing significant challenges.

Do any of these apply to you? By identifying what you're hiding, you can begin to understand its impact on your life and take steps toward a more authentic existence.

HIDING INVENTORY

Now, your turn. Check the boxes next to the aspects of yourself you may be hiding or have hidden at any point in your life.

Personal Identity and Background

☐ Accent   ☐ Race
☐ Age   ☐ Sexual Orientation
☐ Education   ☐ Socioeconomic Status
☐ Ethnicity   ☐ Speech
☐ Gender Identity

Health and Wellness

☐ Addiction   ☐ Mental Health
☐ Body Image   ☐ Neurodiversity
☐ Disabilities: ☐ Physical Appearance
   Non-Apparent   ☐ Trauma
☐ Disabilities: Apparent   ☐ Weight
☐ Medical Diagnosis

Finances

☐ Bankruptcy   ☐ Wealth Abundance
☐ Debt
☐ Income

Family and Relationships

- ☐ Family Challenges
- ☐ Fertility Issues
- ☐ Parental Status
- ☐ Relationship Status
- ☐ Sexual Experiences
- ☐ Personal Beliefs and Interests
- ☐ Interests/Hobbies

Personal Beliefs

- ☐ Politics
- ☐ Religious Beliefs

Professional Life and Aspirations

- ☐ Career Setbacks
- ☐ Dreams
- ☐ Failures
- ☐ Professional Aspirations
- ☐ Other:

_____

<u>Note</u>: You are not alone on this path. Hiding is an experience that most of us share, with many people hiding multiple facets of their lives. As you progress through this book, keep this list handy—new memories and realizations may emerge, deepening your understanding of your own experiences with hiding.

THE ELEMENTS OF HIDING

It Turns Out Hiding Is Universal

As I delved deeper into learning about the phenomenon of hiding, I discovered a universal truth: everyone hides something. This idea is not new; sociologist Erving Goffman coined the term "covering" in 1963, describing how individuals adjust their identities to fit social norms. This concept became even clearer to me through Dr. Christie Smith and Kenji Yoshino's groundbreaking 2013 work on "covering" with Deloitte, which highlighted how pervasive these behaviors are across cultures and workplaces. Understanding that hiding is a widespread issue, not just my personal struggle, was a game changer for me. It ignited my passion to keep understanding why people hide and emphasized the importance of creating a framework for "unhiding" and building connection.

In a 2023 follow-up study, "Uncovering Culture," with the Deloitte University Leadership Center for Inclusion, Smith and Yoshino's findings revealed that 60 percent of people reported hiding aspects of themselves at work, a very slight decrease from 61 percent a decade earlier in the authors' 2013 "Uncovering Talent" report. Statistics from their updated 2019 report went even deeper, highlighting hiding among certain groups in the workplace:

- 83 percent of LGBTQIA individuals
- 66 percent of women
- 67 percent of women of color
- 61 percent of people with disabilities
- 45 percent of straight, white men

When I share these findings, people always react with, *"Those numbers are way off; it's more like 100%. Everyone is hiding something."* Just consider the last few years: With cameras off, muted microphones, and blurred backgrounds, many people use virtual barriers to make hiding the norm, allowing us to keep our true selves hidden more than ever before. That said, we rarely take time to reflect on what we conceal and how it affects our relationships and sense of connection.

I challenge you throughout this book to engage in what I call "self-centered work," that deep introspection and curiosity about yourself and those around you. I invite you to examine your own layers—yourself, your family, your workplace, and your community. Because if it is true that 100 percent of people are hiding, then you need to ask yourself: What am I hiding? What are others around me hiding? These are the actions you can take when you want to build deeper connections and enhance your understanding through greater awareness.

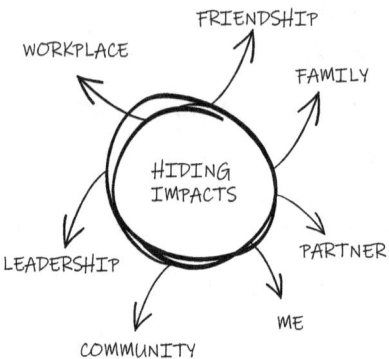

The Cost of Hiding

Hiding affects nearly every aspect of your life. At its core, hiding acts as a shield against emotional or physical threats, driven by a fear of rejection and judgment. This fear, often deeply ingrained in your self-concept, leads you to believe that if others knew "the real you," they might turn away, reject you, or retaliate. According to psychologist Carl Rogers, this fear impacts how you interact with the world, affecting your relationships, mental health, and overall well-being. By hiding, we sacrifice authenticity and connection, leading to emotional exhaustion and isolation.

Shame plays a big role in this fear, whispering—and often shouting—that something is wrong with you or that you are so flawed that you must hide those aspects of yourself at all costs. This negative self-view is typically rooted in early experiences and reinforced by societal norms that impose rigid standards about what is acceptable, desirable, and "normal." Understanding these psychological underpinnings can help individuals begin to address and overcome their fears.

Feeling Isolated: Hiding leads to strong feelings of isolation, even when surrounded by people. It creates an invisible barrier that prevents genuine intimacy and connection.

Stifled Growth: When you hide, you limit your personal and professional growth. The energy spent on maintaining a façade could be redirected towards embracing opportunities and achieving your true potential.

Health Consequences: The constant stress of hiding can manifest in physical health issues such as chronic fatigue, headaches, and weakened immune function, alongside mental health challenges like anxiety and depression.

Impact on Performance: Hiding undermines your performance. It diminishes engagement, creativity, and innovation, leading to a decrease in satisfaction and overall productivity.

Loss of Self-Esteem: The more you hide, the more

you reinforce the belief that your true self is unacceptable. This erosion of self-esteem can lead to a cycle of further hiding and increased self-doubt.

Barrier to Authentic Relationships: Authentic relationships require vulnerability and openness. By hiding, you prevent others from truly knowing you, which limits the depth of your relationships and creates superficial connections.

RESEARCH

For those of you who need some data, research by John E. Pachankis in Psychological Bulletin (2007) and Anna-Kaisa Newheiser and Manuela Barreto in the Journal of Experimental Social Psychology (2014) found that individuals who hide aspects of their identity report higher levels of loneliness and lower well-being. Maintaining a façade demands constant vigilance and immense psychological energy, often leading to anxiety, depression, or disconnection. Over time, this suppression of your authentic self can lead to burnout—a state of emotional, physical, and mental exhaustion caused by prolonged stress.

In relationships, hiding prevents genuine intimacy and connection. When you hide parts of yourself, your interactions often lack a certain level of depth and can lead to isolation and misunderstanding, even among family, friends, or colleagues. When you are hiding, every moment and movement are carefully planned to avoid being discovered. This continuous effort to hide stops you from forming deeper connections and being your fullest self. It impacts authenticity which is crucial for trust and strong relationships—vital for teamwork and collaboration. Diane Quinn and Stephenie Chaudoir in the *Journal of Personal Social Psychology* (2009) found that people with hidden stigmas struggle to form deep connections because they fear being exposed.

Recent research highlights that hiding who you are at work has many negative effects. It impacts feelings of belonging, weakens leadership, reduces engagement, and increases loneliness and stress. Employees who hide parts of themselves feel more tired and isolated, which makes them feel less connected to their workplace according to *Human Resource Management Review* by Robyn A. Berkeley and colleagues (2019) and Deloitte's *Uncovering Culture (2023)*. This effort to cover also affects the ability to lead and be productive, causing more burnout and lower job performance. To address these issues, research has found that workplaces need to be more inclusive and supportive of diverse identities. This inclusivity improves retention, engagement, and innovation, ultimately benefiting the bottom line and making a strong business case for unhiding.

A Case Study

After a presentation, a man approached me as the line of attendees with questions dwindled. I noticed his nervousness. He sighed, a mixture of relief and apprehension in his eyes.

"I really appreciate that you included people hiding their accents and stutters among the list of things people hide. I don't speak in meetings," he admitted. "I'm worried about my accent. People will think I'm not smart, or they'll dismiss my ideas."

Curious, I asked, "Has this happened before? Have you felt judged or rejected?"

"Yes, it has," he replied, his voice tinged with frustration. "Sometimes, when I've spoken up, I've seen it—the quick glances, the slight frowns, the sighs. It makes me think they're judging me. It's just easier to stay quiet."

I leaned in, understanding the weight of his struggle, "And how do you think this affects your work and your team?"

"It's holding me back," he confessed. "I have ideas, good ones, but I don't share them. I worry people

won't understand me. I worry about not being seen as a team player or not fitting the culture here. It's lonely and, honestly, exhausting."

This story highlights the profound impact of hiding at work in three ways:

- ***Personal Impact:*** He feels stressed, anxious, and stuck in his job because he's always worried about being judged. This constant fear makes him tired and lonely, causing him to hold back his ideas.

- ***Team Impact:*** His team misses out on his good ideas, experiences reduced teamwork and communication, and may wrongly assume he's not a team player or doesn't fit the culture. This creates a workplace atmosphere where people don't feel included or valued.

- ***Leadership Impact:*** Leaders may overlook him for answers or innovation and may not see him as promotable.

Hiding here presents itself as a lose-lose situation.

Over time, suppressing your best self can result in emotional exhaustion, disengagement, and even apathy. Have you ever felt the cost of hiding?

THE BENEFITS OF HIDING

It's important to mention that despite its significant drawbacks, hiding isn't all bad. Sometimes, it can protect you, help you focus, and keep you safe. Knowing when to hide and when to share can be empowering. It's about having choice and control over when you reveal and when you don't.

- A project manager and mother of two rarely discusses her family life with her colleagues. "I'm scared of missing out on promotions if they think I'm too busy at home or care too much about my kids."

- After being diagnosed with a chronic illness, one person chose not to disclose their condition at work. "I'm worried about how it might change the way I'm treated or even my job security."

- "In this office, it feels like you're walking on eggshells with anything politically related. No one knows my politics," one woman who is a lawyer says quietly.

- "I've learned it's better not to share too much around here," a man who is an accountant says, "My boss doesn't see the relevance of personal issues at work. It makes it hard to be open when you know it won't be received well."

Hiding can provide safety, serving as a buffer against potential risks until you feel more secure. In professional settings, this might mean withholding personal opinions until you better understand the landscape or can trust your audience's receptivity. This careful management of self-disclosure helps you maintain control over your personal boundaries, protecting your emotional well-being; I call it 'strategic hiding.'

Strategic hiding can also help you focus on tasks without the distraction of personal issues, particularly in high-stakes situations, where it may be critical to maximize respect and influence. For example, you might choose to keep certain aspects of your personal life private during a critical project or while navigating office politics, ensuring that your professional contributions are the primary focus.

However, even with its benefits, 'strategic hiding' can still take a toll on your well-being and sense of connection to yourself and others. It remains exhausting and lonely. Continually managing what you share and what you conceal can drain your energy and create a sense of isolation, as you're not fully able to be yourself.

Reflection: Recognizing the roots of our hiding behavior is the first step toward overcoming it. As you explore these concepts, consistently ask yourself: ***How is hiding holding me back from thriving and connecting?***

Closing Insight: In both personal and professional environments, you often navigate the delicate balance between revealing and concealing aspects of yourself. How much should you share, and what should remain private? How frequently do you take time to be curious and reflective? These decisions shape your interactions, relationships, and, ultimately, your self-perception. Start your journey of self-discovery by identifying one thing you typically hide about yourself and examine why you do that. Understanding the root causes of your hiding behaviors is the first step toward meaningful change.

Next steps

To gain a deeper understanding of why we hide and how we can unhide, it is instructive to explore the different archetypes that represent various hiding behaviors. This exploration can reveal insights into our actions and help us on our path to authenticity.

NOTES

PART TWO

Understanding The Four Archetypes

In this section, we explore the four archetypes of hiding: *The Guardian, The Wonderer, The Open Book, and The Fortress*. Each chapter is dedicated to one archetype, helping you identify which resonates most with your experiences. Through a self-guided quiz, stories, and reflection questions, you will gain a deeper understanding of your hiding behaviors and how they shape your interactions with the world.

Each archetype chapter includes eight key components to guide you:

- **Matrix of Curiosity and Revealing**: Understand where each archetype falls on the scale of curiosity and openness.
- **Guiding Story**: Read a narrative that exemplifies the archetype in action.
- **Signature Phrase**: Learn common phrases associated with each archetype and how to recognize them.
- **Key Characteristics**: Identify the main traits that define each archetype.
- **Psychological Dynamics**: Explore the underlying psychological mechanisms that drive each archetype's behavior.
- **Graphic Highlighting Key Considerations**: Visual representation of important aspects to consider for each archetype.
- **Reflection**: Engage with questions designed to prompt self-reflection and deeper understanding.
- **Closing Insights**: Gain final thoughts and actionable takeaways for each archetype.

CHAPTER 2

What Type of Hider Are You?

Explore the ways you hide. To better understand the hidden aspects of who we are, we can look at four archetypes that represent the different ways that we conceal our true selves. A self-guided quiz helps identify your predominant hiding type, uncovering hidden fears, desires, and defenses that shape your interactions with the world.

Matrix of Curiosity and Revealing for Archetypes

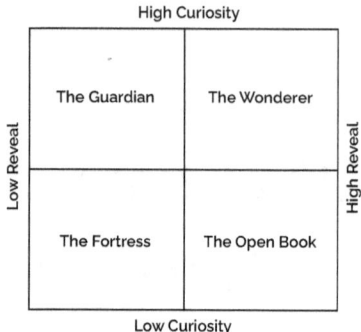

Meet the four archetypes:

- **The Guardian:** Protects secrets and vulnerabilities, creating a sense of security through concealment.
- **The Wonderer:** Seeks new experiences to avoid deep self-reflection, hiding behind a façade of curiosity.
- **The Open Book:** Shares some things openly to mask deeper insecurities, using transparency as a shield.
- **The Fortress:** Builds emotional walls to keep others at a distance, hiding through isolation and level of detachment.

QUIZ: DISCOVER YOUR HIDING TYPE

Let's take a moment to gain insights into your own behavior and how it shapes your interactions with the world.

This quiz will help you understand how you deal with personal challenges, manage your private life, and interact with others.

Instructions:

Rate each statement on the next page from 1 (Strongly Disagree) to 5 (Strongly Agree). Your scores will reveal which type of hider you predominantly are: *The Guardian, The Wonderer, The Open Book,* or *The Fortress.*

_____ 1. When faced with personal challenges, I prefer to keep them to myself.

_____ 2. I often wonder if there are parts of my personality that I keep hidden from others.

_____ 3. I feel comfortable sharing details about my personal life with others.

_____ 4. I find it difficult and uncomfortable to explore or discuss my feelings and fears, even with close family or friends.

_____ 5. I worry that people will treat me differently if they know everything about me.

_____ 6. I actively seek feedback and insights to better understand my true nature.

_____ 7. I believe that being an "open book" helps avoid misunderstandings and builds stronger relationships.

_____ 8. The idea of change or personal growth is more intimidating than exciting.

_____ 9. I have a part of my identity that I feel I need to hide to succeed in my career.

_____ 10. I am constantly curious about how to align my actions more closely with my inner values.

_____ 11. People often tell me that I share too much information too soon.

_____ 12. I prefer to keep things as they are rather than delve into new self-explorations or make changes.

Scoring Guide:

Sum the scores for the questions aligned with each archetype:

- **The Guardian:** Questions 1, 5, 9
  Total: _____
- **The Wonderer:** Questions 2, 6, 10
  Total: _____
- **The Open Book:** Questions 3, 7, 11
  Total: _____
- **The Fortress:** Questions 4, 8, 12
  Total: _____

The archetype with the <u>highest</u> total score indicates your predominant hiding type.

Next Steps

Let's learn more about each type:

- The Guardian (Chapter 3)
- The Wonderer (Chapter 4)
- The Open Book (Chapter 5)
- The Fortress (Chapter 6)

The insights these chapters contain will help you understand yourself and others better.

The Guardian

Protecting Secrets and Revealing Truths

Are you someone who tries to live as their true self, but also keeps some secrets? The Guardian protects vulnerabilities through concealment, leading to an internal struggle between maintaining a façade and seeking authenticity. Learn how embracing vulnerability can enhance personal growth and relationships.

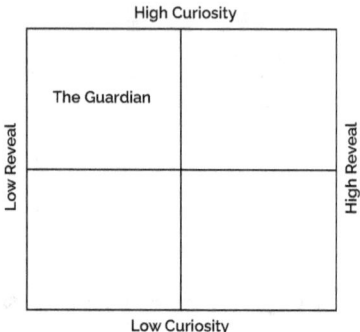

THE GUARDIAN: HIGH CURIOSITY, LOW REVEAL

Story Introduction: On a recent flight, I sit next to a graphic designer. As our conversation moves beyond small talk, I share my mission of encouraging leaders to help their employees stop hiding and explain how I hid my hand for twenty-five years. Something I say strikes a chord with him; his posture shifts and he lowers his head.

He hesitates, then leans in slightly, lowering his voice as if to shield his words from the rest of the airplane cabin. "I know exactly what you're talking about. I hide," he confesses, his eyes not meeting mine. "I never tell anyone this, but I didn't go to college. Whenever it comes up, I just want to leave the room."

As the plane engines hum in the background, he continues, "I'm so afraid that if people knew, they'd think less of me, doubt my abilities, not see the success I've built, but only the degree I never got. It's exhausting to always be worried."

Signature Phrase: "I hide. I'm afraid if someone finds out they will judge or reject me. It's better to keep hiding."

Characteristics

- **Protectiveness:** Tends to conceal aspects of themselves to avoid judgment.
- **Cautiousness:** Carefully manages the boundary between public and private self.
- **Curiosity:** Intrigued that something could be different if they stopped hiding.

Psychological Dynamics

Guardians often experience an internal struggle between the desire to reveal their true selves and the need to maintain a protective façade. This tension can lead to anxiety and self-protective behavior, resulting in feelings of loneliness and disconnection.

- **Internal Conflict:** Balancing the need to hide with the desire for authenticity.

- **Anxiety:** Fear of exposure and judgment, leading to protective behaviors.
- **Isolation:** Tendency to disconnect from others to maintain privacy.

Hiding Behavior	Short-Term Benefits	Long-Term Impacts
Concealing education	Avoids immediate judgment	Ongoing fear of exposure, limits career opportunities
Not sharing personal struggles at work	Maintains professional image	Builds internal stress, reduces genuine connections
Avoiding social events	Reduces anxiety in the moment	Leads to loneliness and missed networking opportunities
Downplaying achievements	Avoids appearing boastful	Lowers self-esteem, misses recognition opportunities
Keeping health issues private	Avoids perceived pity or judgment	Increases isolation, prevents receiving support

The graphic illustrates examples of hiding behaviors of The Guardian archetype, highlighting the short-term benefits and long-term impacts of these behaviors.

Reflection

1. **Reflect on a Time:** Remember a moment when you felt the need to hide a part of yourself. What were you protecting, and why?

2. **Personal Connection:** Can you think of a time you saw someone else behaving like The Guardian? How did this impact their relationships or professional development?

3. **The Cost of Guarding:** Consider the emotional

and physical toll of maintaining a guarded persona. What might be the costs? Can you connect any personal health or wellness issues to periods of increased secrecy?

Closing Insight: Embracing Vulnerability as Strength

For Guardians, revealing their inner self is daunting but rewarding. By understanding your instincts to protect yourself and gently challenging them, you can begin to enjoy the benefits of more meaningful connections and authenticity. Whether in personal relationships or professional settings, every step toward openness enriches your interactions, boosting your sense of belonging and fulfillment. Let this chapter serve as your guide and companion as you navigate the delicate balance between protection and expression, moving toward a more authentic self.

NEXT STEPS

Now that we know The Guardian, let's meet The Wonderer. The Wonderer is curious and always tries to understand more about themselves. This attitude can help people in this category grow and connect better with others.

CHAPTER 4

The Wonderer

Curiosity and Making Connection

Are you someone who loves learning about themselves and is naturally open with others? The Wonderer's curiosity helps them make deep connections. They engage in deep self-reflection, enhancing self-awareness and fostering meaningful connections. Balancing curiosity with privacy is crucial for personal growth.

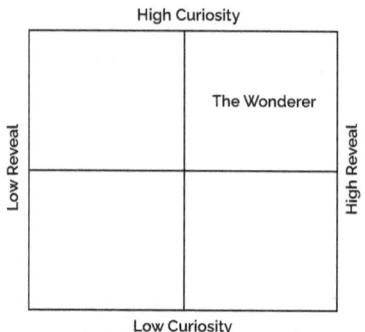

THE WONDERER: HIGH CURIOSITY, HIGH REVEAL

Story Introduction: "What am I hiding?" she asks me on our video call, a spark of curiosity in her eyes as we discuss self-awareness. Her questions start a deeper conversation about the parts of herself she keeps private, like her child's mental health history, which she rarely shares.

As we continue to talk, she explores why she chooses to share some things and not others. "Why do I not share this? What stories have I told myself about why this part of my life must stay hidden? What might change if I were more open about it?"

Encouraging her to think about the benefits of opening up, I suggest, "Talking about your challenges can invite support and deepen connections. It's not about revealing everything to everyone; rather, it's important to consider if sharing could bring you closer to others. What might you gain from being a little more open?"

Signature Phrase: "What am I hiding?"

Characteristics

- **Curiosity:** Asks questions to understand oneself and others better.
- **Openness:** Willingness to explore and reveal personal aspects to deepen connections.
- **Introspection:** Engages in deep self-reflection to uncover hidden desires, fears, and traits.

Psychological Dynamics

As a Wonderer, your introspective nature often leads you to look within, uncovering hidden aspects of yourself. This journey of self-discovery enhances self-awareness and helps reconcile internal conflicts, leading to more meaningful connections.

- **Self-Awareness:** Discovering and understanding hidden parts of yourself.
- **Reconciliation:** Integrating different parts of your personality.

- **Empathy:** Forming deep, meaningful connections through understanding and openness.

Area of Curiosity	Examples	Benefits
Personal Hobbies	Exploring new hobbies like painting, hiking, or cooking.	Enhances creativity, provides relaxation and self-expression.
Professional Interests	Learning new skills, attending workshops, networking.	Promotes career growth, opens new opportunities, and builds professional connections.
Social Interactions	Engaging in diverse social groups, volunteering.	Expands social network, fosters empathy, and builds community.
Intellectual Pursuits	Reading books, taking online courses, attending lectures.	Deepens knowledge, stimulates intellectual growth, and satisfies curiosity.
Spiritual Exploration	Meditation, attending religious or spiritual gatherings.	Promotes inner peace, self-awareness, and spiritual growth.

The chart outlines the areas of curiosity, provides illustrative examples, and highlights the benefits of exploration.

Reflection

1. **Journey of Self-Discovery:** What questions have you asked yourself during your journey of self-discovery? What surprising things have you learned about yourself?

2. **Insight from Feedback:** Discuss a time when feedback led to a significant insight into or change in your perspective.

3. **The Wonderer's Challenge:** How can Wonderers

maintain their integrity in environments that discourage vulnerability and diverse perspectives?

Closing Insight: Curiosity as the Gateway to Growth

As a Wonderer, your journey of introspection and discovery is crucial, filled with potential for immense joy and fulfillment. Approach each step with courage and curiosity, letting your discoveries enrich every aspect of your life.

NEXT STEPS

Now that we know The Wonderer, let's look at The Open Book. The Open Book highlights the complexities of sharing too much and the importance of balancing openness with privacy.

CHAPTER 5

The Open Book

Sharing and Its Challenges

Are you someone who is very open about their life but sometimes struggles with sharing deeper issues? The Open Book often shares extensively to manage perceptions and avoid deeper vulnerabilities. Learn about the challenges of oversharing and find a balance that helps build genuine connections.

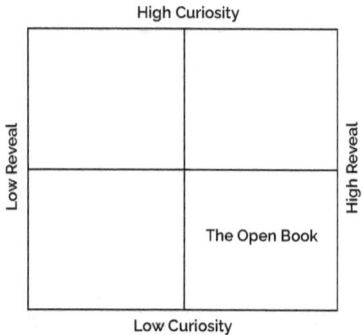

THE OPEN BOOK: LOW CURIOSITY, HIGH REVEAL

Story Introduction: At a recent conference, a woman approaches me with an eager smile. "I loved your talk," she says enthusiastically. "But I'm not really hiding anything. I'm definitely an open book."

Her declaration comes with a light laugh and an air of pride.

She reveals more about her approach to how open she is. "Everyone knows everything about me," she explains. "I give all my opinions. Sometimes, I even wonder if I share too much."

As we talk further, she admits that her transparency has sometimes backfired and caused problems, leading to regret when personal details are used against her or when the line between personal and professional life gets blurry.

Signature Phrase: "I don't hide anything; if anything, I probably way overshare."

Characteristics

- **Transparency:** Openly shares personal details with ease.
- **Oversharing:** Often discloses more than necessary, blurring the lines between their personal and professional life.
- **Control:** Uses openness as a strategy to manage how others perceive them. What they share is often curated.

Psychological Dynamics

As an Open Book, your extensive sharing might be a way to prevent others from seeing your deeper vulnerabilities. This can create a façade of openness that controls how others see you rather than fostering genuine connections. The boundaries between what is shared and what is kept private can often be blurred, leading to several behaviors:

- **Superficial Openness:** Shares a lot often to avoid deeper vulnerabilities.

- **Perception Management:** Controls how others perceive them through strategic sharing.
- **Deflection:** Uses oversharing to distract from more personal feelings.

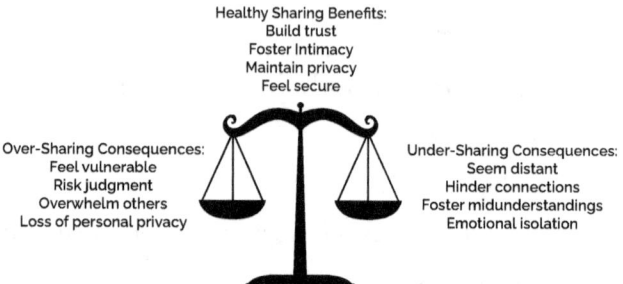

The graphic illustrates the consequences of oversharing, the other side showing the consequences of under-sharing; the middle highlights the benefits of healthy sharing.

Reflection

1. **Balance of Sharing:** Recall a time when sharing something personal led to a positive or negative outcome. What did you learn about the boundaries of sharing?

2. **Value of Transparency:** Reflect on how transparency has played a role in building trust. Can you share a personal story about how being open improved a relationship?

3. **Oversharing:** Have you ever overshared? What

were the consequences, and how did you handle the situation afterward?

Closing Insight: Depth Beyond Disclosure

The journey for The Open Book entails mastering balanced sharing and transforming your interactions into meaningful connections. This skill develops through the mindful practice of evaluating what, when, and how much to share. As you improve, you'll find your relationships in all areas of life becoming richer and more meaningful.

Next Steps

Now that we know The Open Book, let's meet The Fortress. The Fortress keeps many secrets and isn't often curious. Understanding this type will help you see your own barriers and learn to open up more.

CHAPTER 6

The Fortress

Building Walls of Silence

Are you someone who doesn't really like to share and resists "self-help" learning? The Fortress builds emotional walls to protect themselves, which can lead to loneliness and hindered growth. Discover ways to slowly lower these defenses and experience the benefits of openness and deeper connections.

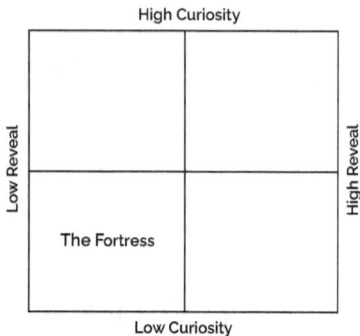

THE FORTRESS: LOW CURIOSITY, LOW REVEAL

Story Introduction: I notice him right away—sitting in the front row, arms crossed, with a skeptical expression. He flips through a copy of my book during a mandatory Diversity, Equity, Inclusion, and Belonging (DEIB) event. Only when another audience member asks, "Do we really need all this personal focus at work?" do I see him smile and nod in agreement, signaling that he, too, prefers to keep personal life and job performance separate.

After the session, he approaches me with cautious curiosity. "I liked your talk, but I'm not convinced it's important in the workplace. Like the other guy said, isn't it better to just focus on business and getting the job done?"

He continues, "I'm not hiding. I just don't think people need to know my business."

I respond, "I hear you. There are definitely boundaries to this, and you're right, at the end of the day, we have to get the work done. And yet, I have found that sharing parts of ourselves can strengthen team dynamics, make people feel more engaged and wanting to contribute, and make us more approachable as leaders."

"And sometimes, even simple acts like listening, remembering details, and being present can have a big impact," I add.

He nods. I'm not sure he's convinced, but the seed is planted.

Signature Phrase: "I'm not hiding. I'm not really sure why this is relevant. It's nobody else's business."

Characteristics

- **Guardedness:** Maintains a protective barrier around personal life.
- **Skepticism:** Doubts the value of personal sharing in professional contexts.
- **Compartmentalization:** Keeps different aspects of life strictly separate.

Psychological Dynamics

As a Fortress, you might resist opening up fully and avoid looking inward. This protective attitude helps you avoid feeling vulnerable but can also hinder your growth and fulfillment. The anxiety about revealing your true self can be intense, prompting you to build higher walls.

- **Protective Attitude:** Maintains a strong, guarded exterior as a defense mechanism against vulnerability.
- **Anxiety:** Fear of judgment or rejection drives the need to hide.
- **Compartmentalization:** Separates personal and professional lives to manage stress and avoid feeling overwhelmed.

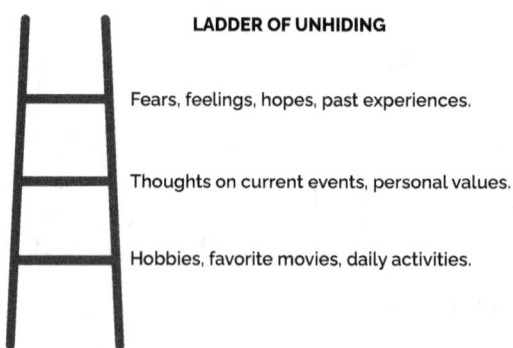

LADDER OF UNHIDING

Fears, feelings, hopes, past experiences.

Thoughts on current events, personal values.

Hobbies, favorite movies, daily activities.

For those identifying with the Fortress archetype, starting to unhide can involve small, layered steps.

Reflection

1. **Breaking Down Walls:** Reflect on a time when you decided to lower your guard. What prompted this change, and how did it impact your relationships or self-perception?

2. **Connecting with Others:** How would you encourage a Fortress (or yourself, if this is you) to open up? Describe techniques or approaches that might be effective.

3. **Understanding Resistance:** Explore the reasons behind your resistance to change or vulnerability. How can understanding these reasons improve your approach?

Closing Insight: Strength in Openness

Being a Fortress can seem advantageous because it allows you to protect yourself from being hurt or judged. By keeping things compartmentalized, you can stay focused on tasks and avoid distractions from personal issues. However, this approach has its downsides, including loneliness and hindered emotional growth, and it may cause others to perceive you as unapproachable, lacking self-awareness, and disconnected.

Learning to open up, even a little, can significantly enhance personal growth and enrich relationships. Embracing vulnerability is a courageous step toward deeper understanding and connection. As you gradually lower your defenses, you'll find that the world can offer support and understanding, and that true strength comes from allowing yourself to be seen and understood. This can lead to more fulfilling connections and a greater sense of belonging.

NEXT STEPS

Now that we know about The Fortress, let's see how the different archetypes mix and affect one another. In the next chapter, we'll explore how these types blend together and shape who we are.

CHAPTER 7

Intersecting Archetypes

There are many sides to who you are. This chapter examines how different hiding archetypes intersect and influence each other. Understanding these intersections helps in navigating personal growth and professional development, leading to a more authentic and fulfilling life.

Exploring Intersections

You are complex. You aren't just one archetype. In truth, you are made up of different traits from each archetype that change over time and in different situations. Understanding this helps in both personal growth and professional development.

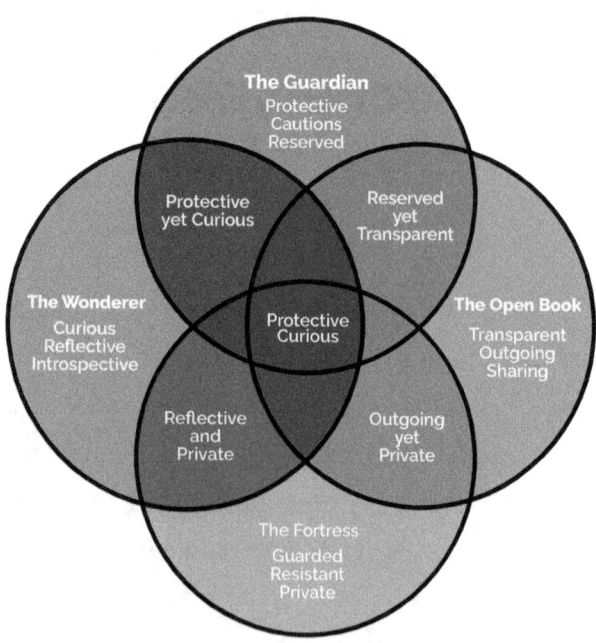

The diagram shows the intersections between archetypes.

Key Intersections:

- **The Guardian and The Wonderer:** Balances privacy with a curiosity for growth. This helps maintain personal boundaries while pursuing growth. Unhiding here can lead to stronger bonds with those you trust, providing a secure support network.

- **The Open Book and The Fortress:** Shares professional successes openly but keeps personal challenges private. This balance maintains a professional image while protecting your personal life. Unhiding here can enhance your credibility while also allowing for deeper, more authentic connections with others.

- **The Open Book and The Wonderer:** Moves from sharing openly to thinking deeply about what and why they share. This helps in roles like mentoring. Unhiding in this intersection can lead to more thoughtful and impactful connections, encouraging deeper understanding and growth.

- **The Fortress and The Guardian:** Keeps most people at a distance while sharing personal details with trusted friends. This careful balance allows safe vulnerability. Unhiding here can lead to stronger bonds with those you trust, providing a secure support network.

- **The Guardian and The Open Book:** Protects vulnerable parts while sharing freely to manage perceptions. This blend allows control over what is revealed. Unhiding here can improve your relationships by fostering transparency while maintaining necessary boundaries.

- **The Wonderer and The Fortress:** Balances curiosity and protection. Seeks new knowledge while keeping strong defenses. Unhiding here can help you balance your curiosity with self-protection, leading to more informed and secure explorations.

Understanding these intersections can help you navigate personal and professional environments more effectively. Embrace your complex identity to boost fulfillment and strengthen relationships.

Reflection

1. **Archetype Evolution:** How might your archetype change over time? How do cultural backgrounds influence these changes?

2. **Balancing Identities:** Reflect on a specific instance when you balanced different parts of your identity,

such as a time when you were at work or in a particular social setting. How did this experience impact your sense of authenticity and connection with others?

3. **Empathy and Inclusivity:** How can sharing your experiences build understanding and inclusivity in your community?

Closing Insight: Embrace the Spectrum of Selves

Approach this journey with curiosity and an open heart. Navigating through different archetypes helps you to handle life's challenges creatively and adaptively—a true strength. As you commit to your growth, you'll discover that your connections with others and your potential for development in all areas of life will significantly increase. Embrace the complexities of your identity to boost your fulfillment and strengthen your relationships, enhancing your personal and professional life. You might find that you embody aspects of all four archetypes at different times, reflecting the multifaceted nature of your experiences. Consider writing a journal entry on how these identities interact and what conflicts they may create.

NEXT STEPS

Now that you know how different aspects and parts of
who you are can mix, let's use some tools to help you
unhide. In the next chapter, you'll learn ways to unhide
that fit each type. This will help you to safely become
your true self and connect better with others. Let's find
out how to take these steps together—but first, a reflection exercise!

REFLECTION EXERCISE: JOURNEY LINE, MAPPING YOUR PERSONAL AND PROFESSIONAL GROWTH

During a "fireside chat," an interview-style conversation aimed at fostering open dialogue and authentic sharing, an executive talked about his layered experiences of identity and hiding with me and the audience. Openly identifying as LGBTQ+ and actively participating in community advocacy and his business resource group, PRIDE, he embodies confidence and authenticity in this aspect of his life. However, he confesses a stark contrast in that confidence when it comes to his educational background.

"I grew up in a low-income neighborhood and attended community college. I'm always worried during interviews and in executive meetings that if I mention this, they'll think less of me," he explains. "I always avoid talking about my education; I hide it."

This example shows how people can be open and confident in one part of their life and may hide other parts of who they are because they are afraid of being judged or treated unfairly.

Reflect on your own journey. When have you felt like

you had to hide parts of yourself? (Refer back to page 14 for the hiding checklist.)

Exploring these behaviors through the lens of the four archetypes—The Guardian, The Wonderer, The Open Book, and The Fortress—further enriches this self-discovery process. This exercise will help you understand why you hide and prepare you for the journey of unhiding.

Exercise: Create Your Journey Line

Map your personal and professional growth, which will help you better understand the moments that have shaped you.

1. **Draw a Line**: On a piece of paper, draw a horizontal line. This will represent your life from past to present.

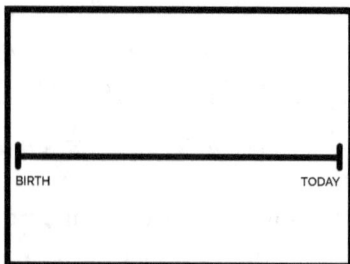

2. **Mark Moments**: Identify times you felt the need to hide parts of yourself. Mark these on the line.

3. **Reflect**: For each marked moment, consider:
   - Why did you hide?
   - How did it impact your relationships and feelings?
   - How did it shape who you are today?
   - How do different aspects of your identity intersect and influence what you choose to hide or reveal?
   - When were you The Guardian, The Wonderer, The Open Book, or The Fortress?

NOTES

PART THREE

Unhiding

In this section, we focus on practical strategies for unhiding. Here, you'll find a four-step framework *(Acknowledge, Invite, Build, Share)* to guide you through the process of embracing your best self. This section includes actionable steps tailored to each archetype, ensuring that the guidance is relevant and effective for your unique journey. Additionally, you'll learn how to apply these principles in both personal and professional contexts, creating a more authentic and inclusive environment around you.

Unhiding Defined

In my first book, *Singlehandedly (2022)*, I defined "unhiding" as follows:

- Connecting outward and sharing the most vulnerable parts of ourselves with others.
- Having courage and taking risks with psychological safety.
- Being seen, accepted, and authentic.
- Recognizing that our differences are our gifts that make us unique and beautiful ... offering perspective and the ability to transcend challenges.
- Building understanding and empathy for someone else's challenges.

Synonyms: *uncovering, sharing, finding freedom, coming out, owning your difference*

Since then, I have deepened my understanding of unhiding to add the following:

- Unhiding is more than a personal release—it's a powerful tool that fosters inclusion and empathy. When you unhide, you invite others into your life, thus deepening relationships, enriching conversations, and encouraging others to open up.

- Unhiding can bring great relief and joy, making you feel more free. It allows you to drop the burdens you've been carrying, reclaim your time, and improve your connections. This process expands your awareness of the world and your inner self, helping you live a more authentic and connected life.

- Unhiding comes with privilege. The ability to openly express personal aspects of yourself without fear of negative consequences is directly influenced by your environment and the support systems around you. Not everyone has the same freedom to unhide safely. Unhiding also has different cultural implications, as societal norms and cultural contexts can greatly influence how and what we choose to reveal.

CHAPTER 8

Unhiding in Your Personal Life

How can you unhide in your personal life? Unhiding is about more than just revealing secrets; it's about embracing your true self and fostering genuine connections. This chapter provides practical tools and strategies, including a four-step framework *(Acknowledge, Invite, Build, Share)* to help you unhide.

STORIES OF UNHIDING

While hiding can feel like holding your breath, unhiding feels like an amazing exhale—a release, a freedom, a bridge to connection, a strategy for thriving. The stories below illustrate the power of unhiding and the profound impact it can have on our lives.

Unhiding involves reframing your stories and finding peace and self-acceptance. Your differences make you unique and strong, pushing you to think outside the box. They help you understand your trauma and turn past pain into strength. For me, it wasn't just about accepting my limb difference. I had to learn to incorporate my hand into my whole identity, which required focusing on it and intentionally finding ways to integrate it into my life. This meant challenging and repatterning the negative, internal voices, finding connection and support from others, and integrating those parts to become whole.

Addiction: *I've been hiding my addiction for twenty years. [Unhiding has] made me reflect on my childhood, my relationships, and what I've been missing by not sharing this part of me. I'm scared of judgment and rejection, but hiding has kept me isolated and controlled. Now that I've voiced it, I'm confronting how this secrecy affects my life and* relationships, and exploring how to use this realization to find support and make better choices for my future.

Disability: *I'm an open book; everyone knows everything about me. But I was hired via Zoom and haven't shared with my team or my manager that I can't walk and am paralyzed from the legs down. I'm terrified that if someone finds out, they'll see me differently and feel compelled to make special accommodations. However, I decided to share my situation with my manager first and then my team. To my surprise, their response was supportive and respectful, and they admired my strength and transparency. This has led to me feeling more included and increased my sense of belonging at work. I feel seen and heard.*

Oversharing: *I share everything with my staff—my weekend activities, my current divorce struggles, and even my parents' passing. I wonder if sharing so much makes us closer or if it is too much for my team. After reflecting on my sharing habits, I realized that setting some boundaries would help maintain professionalism while still being authentic. I started to share selectively, focusing on stories that build team morale and trust without oversharing personal struggles. This approach has strengthened my professional relationships and increased mutual respect among my team members. Now, I am working on setting boundaries* and managing how much I overshare with friends and family. It's a work in progress.

Parenting Challenges: *I keep my camera off and my mic muted when I work from home to shield my daughter's outbursts; I'm protecting her. I don't want anyone to think I'm a bad leader or a terrible parent if they hear what's happening. However, I realized some people in my inner circle would benefit from knowing more about me. I started to share a bit about my home situation with close colleagues, explaining the challenges I face. This honesty has fostered deeper connections and understanding, and my colleagues have been incredibly supportive, offering help and flexibility when needed. Some of my colleagues also shared their own challenges with their children, which made me feel less isolated and more connected.*

Mental Health: *At work, I maintain a confident and composed exterior and freely share my professional achievements and strategies with my colleagues, earning their admiration and trust. However, I carefully guard my struggles with anxiety, sharing them only with my closest friends. This allows me to maintain my professional image while protecting my vulnerabilities. Recently, I decided to share my anxiety struggles with a select group of people during a mental health awareness meeting at work. The response was overwhelmingly positive, with many colleagues expressing* *their support and sharing their own experiences. This has created a more open and supportive environment. It feels like a huge weight has been lifted.*

Professional Vulnerability: *I eagerly take on challenging projects and enjoy learning new programming languages. However, when I encounter criticism or feel my work is under scrutiny, I retreat and become very protective of my ideas. I might work on innovative projects in isolation, only sharing them with my team once I feel confident that they are flawless and ready for feedback. This allows me to satisfy my curiosity while protecting myself from potential rejection. Recently, I started to share my ideas earlier in the process with a few trusted colleagues. This has not only provided valuable feedback that improved my projects but also helped me build stronger professional relationships.*

As these stories emphasize, vulnerability and authenticity are important in building stronger, more meaningful relationships and connections with ourselves and others. Remember, you don't have to do this alone—or singlehandedly. Unhiding is a collective journey that benefits from shared experiences and mutual support.

A FOUR-STEP UNHIDING FRAMEWORK

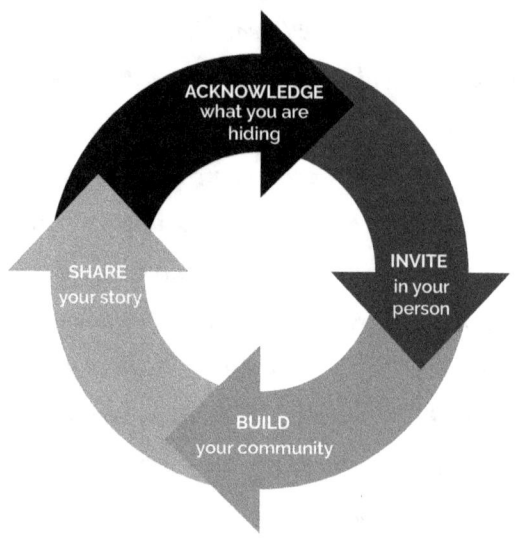

I have identified four critical steps to unhiding—
Acknowledge, Invite, Build, and *Share*—which serve as a
guide for learning to embrace your uniqueness and lower
your guard. These steps are not just theoretical concepts
but actionable strategies crucial for personal growth.
Implementing them requires a structured approach to
ensure meaningful and lasting change.

1. **Acknowledge:** Identify what you're hiding, reflect
   on how it's holding you back or adding value, and
   determine your archetype. Pause and create space
   for introspection.

Example: Someone feels isolated in their social circle because they hide their struggle with anxiety. They acknowledge their anxiety by journaling about their feelings and recognizing how it affects their interactions with friends.

2. **Invite in a Trusted Friend:** Choose carefully whom to involve in your personal journey. Look for empathetic, curious, trustworthy listeners. Pause and create space for questions.

   Example: After acknowledging their anxiety, they decide to invite a close friend into their journey. They choose a friend who has always shown empathy and trustworthiness. During a calm moment, they share their struggle with anxiety, explaining how it has impacted their social interactions. They ask the friend for support and understanding, inviting them to ask questions and be part of their journey towards openness.

3. **Build Community:** Seek out people with shared experiences—whether you find them in online groups, support networks, or employee resource groups (ERGs) in your workplace. Building this community helps you realize you aren't alone and

validates your experiences. Pause and create space for questions.

Example: Encouraged by the support from their friend, they seek out a local support group for individuals with anxiety. They attend meetings, share their experiences, and listen to others' stories. This connection with people who understand their struggle helps them feel less isolated and more supported. They get curious and seek out and join an online forum where they can discuss anxiety openly and seek advice from others.

4. **Share:** Tell your story so that others can see themselves in your experiences, encouraging them to start their journey of self-discovery and self-awareness. Pause and create space for questions.

   Example: With growing confidence from their new community, they decide to share their journey more broadly. They write a post on social media about their struggle with anxiety, detailing their path from isolation to finding support. They encourage others who might be hiding their own struggles to reach out for help and share their experiences. This act of sharing not only educates their social circle but also inspires others to start their own journeys of unhiding. It also invites others to learn more about anxiety and raises awareness.

The Four Steps create a powerful loop, a flywheel of change. Sharing your story sets off a chain reaction, inspiring others to be brave and start their unhiding journey. As more people join in, communities become more open and accepting. This shared journey builds a supportive and genuine space, where the cycle of sharing and inclusion grows stronger. This transformation encourages people to be authentic and feel included, and creates spaces that value different experiences and perspectives.

STARTING THE CONVERSATION

Starting the conversation about hiding can be challenging, but it's an important step toward building deeper connections and fostering authenticity. One strategy I often recommend is to begin by sharing your inspiration.

You might say, "I'm reading this book about hiding and how it affects our lives, our relationships, and our performance. The author shared her story of hiding her disability for twenty-five years and mentioned that over 60 percent of us are hiding something in the workplace or other aspects of our lives. This really got me thinking about my life and what I might be hiding. I wanted to share a piece of myself with you." Or use a similar variation that reflects your own thoughts about hiding.

This approach not only opens the door to a meaningful conversation but also sets a tone of vulnerability and trust, encouraging the other person to share as well.

THE PAUSING PRINCIPLE: CREATING SPACE FOR EMPATHY AND UNDERSTANDING

When you invite people to learn what you've been hiding, it's essential to give them the space to react with questions, curiosity, and time to process new information.

Many of you who have lived with your secrets for years, or even your entire lives, often prepare for the moment of revelation, expecting those you confide in to instantly grasp the depth of your sharing and be okay with it.

However, this revelation may be completely unexpected and unfamiliar for your listeners. They haven't walked in your shoes or had the luxury of time to embrace your truths. They may need a moment to comprehend and be curious. Sometimes, their initial reactions may not align with your expectations, but offering them this space to process—a moment to pause—is crucial for fostering a dialogue grounded in empathy.

The pause can feel uncomfortable—incredibly uncomfortable.

Understanding reactions as a natural component of the unhiding process acknowledges your varied starting points. Consider the analogy of watering dry soil: at first, the water merely sits atop it, taking its time to penetrate the surface. Similarly, your revelations may need time to seep into the understanding of your listeners, requiring patience and openness as they absorb the essence of your shared truths. As you examine your own secrets, it's crucial to acknowledge that you also need time to fully comprehend their impact on you.

Pausing creates checkpoints for people to absorb, ask questions, absorb some more, and then ask even more questions—all in a psychologically safe environment. It's about making room for questions, allowing for curiosity with kindness, and creating space for reflection.

Yes, pausing adds time, but it also strengthens your relationships with others (and your relationship with yourself).

Unsure how to react when someone unhides to you?

- Listen.
- Pause.

- Inquire if asking questions from a place of kindness and curiosity would be okay.

Consider these as starting places for follow-up:

- "Tell me more about your experience."
- "How has this journey shaped your daily life?"
- "Is there anything specific you want me to know or understand?"
- "How can I best support you with what you've shared?"

Unhiding is a conversation, not a monologue. By giving space for curiosity and understanding, you create environments where genuine connection and empathy can flourish.

Story: A colleague confides in me about their ongoing battle with Crohn's disease. This is a condition I knew of, but I didn't fully understand the personal impact it could have on someone's life. What stands out to me, however, is how they navigate this "unhiding."

After sharing, they pause, giving me space to process the information. This pause isn't filled with expectation or discomfort but with an invitation for curiosity. They don't quickly jump to another topic; instead, they create space for initial questions, allowing me to ask how the disease affected their daily life and to grasp the nuances of their journey. This approach educates me about their experience and deepens our connection. It is a powerful reminder of how allowing space for questions and understanding can transform a moment of vulnerability into one of bonding and empathy, and it opens the door for me to share parts of myself, creating deeper connection.

STRATEGIES FOR UNHIDING

Unhiding is not an overnight process or the flip of a switch; it requires unlearning the patterns and stories you've told yourself and finding ways to integrate those hidden parts into your whole self. It's about following the steps, doing the work on yourself, and being that person for someone else. By doing so, you pave the way for a more inclusive world where psychological safety is prioritized, inspiring others to do the same.

We are starting to see a cultural shift where mental health and other hidden parts of our lives are coming to light. Celebrities, athletes, and people on social media are sharing their struggles and personal challenges. They are showing us what it looks like to unhide. This openness helps to 'normalize' these conversations and shows that it is okay to be authentic and transparent.

Seeing these examples reduces the stigma around these issues and encourages others to unhide and embrace their full identities. By watching others, we can learn to embrace our hidden parts and foster environments where being authentic is celebrated.

Here are some key strategies you can use to manage the journey effectively.

- **Set Clear Boundaries:** Know what you're comfortable sharing, with whom, and when. This helps you stay professional and feel safe, ensuring you reveal your best self in a good way.

- **Seek Support:** Becoming more open isn't something to do alone. Resources like friends, family, mentors, therapists, or support groups can be really helpful. They can guide you and support you as you share more about yourself.

- **Monitor Reactions:** Pay close attention to how others respond when you share. This feedback is important because it helps you adjust how much you share to make sure it has a positive impact on your goals.

- **Embrace the Power of the Pause:** After sharing, take a moment for others to absorb and reflect on what you've said. Allow for the discomfort. This pause can help others understand and connect with you more deeply.

TAILORED APPROACHES FOR DIFFERENT ARCHETYPES

Archetype	Key Traits	Hiding Behavior	Unhiding Strategy
The Guardian	Protective, Cautious	Keeps certain aspects of self private, fear of rejection and judgment	Gradual disclosure in safe environments, seek supportive listeners
The Wonderer	Curious, Reflective	Pauses to think, often introspective	Open questioning, engage in reflective conversations with trusted individuals
The Open Book	Transparent, Honest	Overshares selectively, lacks boundaries at times	Balanced sharing, set clear boundaries for personal stories
The Fortress	Reserved, Guarded	Builds up emotional walls, keeps personal life hidden, compartmentalizes	Incremental sharing, start with low-risk disclosures and build trust gradually

This chart categorizes four archetypes—The Guardian, The Wonderer, The Open Book, and The Fortress—highlighting their key traits, typical hiding behaviors, and effective strategies for unhiding.

Depending on your archetype, consider these specific approaches to unhide more effectively.

ACTIONABLE STEPS FOR THE GUARDIAN

Daily Reflection Journal

- **What to Do:** Spend ten minutes each evening writing about your day. Focus on moments when you felt the urge to hide something. Describe the situation, your feelings, and the reasons behind your decision.
- **Why:** This will help you become more aware of your hiding patterns and triggers.

Trusted Confidant

- **What to Do:** Identify one person in your life whom you trust deeply. Make a commitment to share one small, hidden aspect of yourself with them each week.
- **Why:** Gradually revealing your true self to a trusted person can reduce the fear of judgment and increase your comfort with vulnerability.

Set Boundaries

- **What to Do:** Clearly define your personal boundaries. Decide what you are comfortable sharing and what you want to keep private. Communicate these boundaries to close friends or family.

- **Why:** Setting boundaries helps you feel secure and in control while allowing you to open up at your own pace.

Mindfulness Meditation

- **What to Do:** Engage in a five-minute mindfulness meditation each morning. Focus on your breath and observe any thoughts or feelings you may have about hiding without judgment.
- **Why:** Mindfulness can reduce anxiety and help you stay present, making it easier to handle situations where you feel the need to hide.

Positive Affirmations

- **What to Do:** Start each day with a positive affirmation such as "I am worthy of being seen and heard." Repeat this affirmation whenever you feel the urge to hide.
- **Why:** Positive affirmations can boost your confidence and remind you of your inherent value.

ACTIONABLE STEPS FOR
THE WONDERER

Curiosity Journal

- **What to Do:** Dedicate ten minutes each day to write down questions you feel compelled to ask yourself. Reflect on these questions and seek answers through reading or conversations.
- **Why:** This activity will encourage deeper self-exploration and personal growth.

Engage in Active Listening

- **What to Do:** During conversations, practice active listening. Focus entirely on the speaker, ask open-ended questions, and refrain from interrupting.
- **Why:** This helps build stronger connections and enhance your understanding of others.

Weekly Reflection

- **What to Do:** Choose one day each week to reflect on what you've learned about yourself and others. Note any changes in your thoughts or behaviors.

- **Why:** Regular reflection helps track personal growth and reinforces learning.

Join a Discussion Group

- **What to Do:** Participate in a book club, workshop, or support group where you can discuss your thoughts and experiences openly.
- **Why:** Sharing insights with others fosters a sense of community and deepens self-awareness.

Personal Development Plan

- **What to Do:** Create a personal development plan outlining your goals for self-discovery and connection. Review and update this plan monthly.
- **Why:** Setting goals and tracking progress ensures continuous personal growth.

ACTIONABLE STEPS FOR THE OPEN BOOK

Think Before You Share

- **What to Do:** Before sharing personal information, pause and ask yourself if it's the right time, place, and audience.
- **Why:** This will help you avoid oversharing and ensure your stories are well received.

Selective Sharing

- **What to Do:** Choose one aspect of your life to keep private and observe how it feels to not share it immediately.
- **Why:** Doing this helps develop boundaries and understand the importance of privacy.

Deep Conversations

- **What to Do:** Schedule regular deep conversations with a close friend or family member where you discuss meaningful topics.
- **Why:** This fosters genuine connection without the need to constantly share personal details.

Journaling for Clarity

- **What to Do:** Write down your thoughts and feelings in a journal instead of immediately sharing them with others.
- **Why:** This can provide a private outlet for your emotions and helps you process your emotions before discussing them with others.

Feedback Loop

- **What to Do:** Ask trusted friends or family members for feedback on your sharing habits. Reflect on their input and adjust accordingly.
- **Why:** Constructive feedback can help you find a balance between openness and privacy.

ACTIONABLE STEPS FOR THE FORTRESS

Small Steps to Sharing

- **What to Do:** Start by sharing small, non-personal details about your day with someone you trust.
- **Why:** This will build the habit of sharing in a low-risk way.

Weekly Check-Ins

- **What to Do:** Schedule a weekly check-in with a friend or family member where you share one thing that's been on your mind.
- **Why:** Doing this provides you with a safe space for opening up gradually.

Explore Your Emotions

- **What to Do:** Spend five minutes each day identifying and naming your emotions. Write them down in a journal.
- **Why:** Recognizing and naming emotions is the first step toward understanding and sharing them.

Join a Support Group

- **What to Do:** Find a local or online support group where people share similar experiences. Start by listening before sharing.
- **Why:** Being part of a supportive community can make it easier to open up over time.

Therapeutic Support

- **What to Do:** Consider seeing a counselor or guide to explore your feelings and learn healthy ways to express them.
- **Why:** Professional guidance can provide the tools and support needed to lower emotional barriers safely.

A PATH TOWARD SELF-ACTUALIZATION

SELF-ACTUALIZATION
morality, creativity,
spontaneity, acceptance,
experience purpose,
meaning and inner potential

SELF-ESTEEM
confidence, achievement, respect of
others, the need to be a unique individual

LOVE AND BELONGING
friendship, family, intimacy, sense of connection

SAFETY AND SECURITY
health, employment, property, family and social abilty

PHYSIOLOGICAL NEEDS
breathing, food, water, shelter, clothing, sleep

Source: SimplyPsychology.org

In the beginning of this book, we discussed how Abraham Maslow's simple hierarchy of needs can guide us toward self-actualization. Unhiding is a crucial step in this journey. By overcoming the barriers at each level of Maslow's pyramid, you not only meet your basic needs but also clear the path to achieving your highest potential. Carl Rogers' theory of self-actualization complements Maslow's, emphasizing that unhiding and embracing your true self is essential for personal growth and realizing your full potential.

Understanding Maslow's Levels and the Impact of Hiding

Maslow's hierarchy of needs shows why unhiding can be so impactful. The pyramid starts with the most basic needs at the bottom and progresses to self-actualization, which resides at the top. As you move up, the adverse effects of hiding become more significant, as do the rewards for unhiding.

Safety: Hiding might seem like a good short-term solution to avoid feeling insecure, but it often leads to long-term anxiety and stress. Acknowledging what you hide begins to address safety concerns.

Example: A person who hides their true career aspirations due to fear of disapproval may feel safe in the short term. However, they will feel stressed and unhappy because they are not following their true passions. By acknowledging their true dreams and unhiding, they can seek opportunities that align with their goals, reducing stress and increasing job satisfaction.

Love and Belonging: Hiding important aspects of your identity can keep you from forming deep and rewarding relationships. Inviting someone to know a secret aspect of you helps foster love and belonging.

Example: A person who hides their cultural background at work to fit in might feel isolated and disconnected from coworkers. By sharing their cultural heritage, they can build stronger, more genuine connections with colleagues, fostering a sense of inclusion and belonging.

Self-Esteem: Constantly hiding can make you feel inadequate or like an imposter. By choosing to unhide, you build genuine self-acceptance and confidence, and it helps you build community.

Example: A professional who hides their creative ideas out of fear of criticism may feel undervalued and lack confidence. By openly sharing their ideas, they can gain recognition and validation from peers, boosting their self-esteem and confidence.

Self-Actualization: At the top of the pyramid, unhiding and sharing your story with others allows you to pursue and realize your full potential. It frees up the energy previously used in hiding.

Example: An artist who, after years of conforming to commercial tastes, decides to create works that are true to their vision might initially face uncertainty. By staying true to their vision, they achieve personal happiness—and, potentially, breakthrough success—realizing their full creative potential.

THE TRANSFORMATIVE POWER OF UNHIDING

As you move through the steps of unhiding, you can start to make significant strides. But what can you expect from this process? Understanding the transformative power of unhiding will highlight the profound impact it can have on your personal and professional life.

Benefits of Unhiding:

- Authentic Relationships
- Increased Self-Acceptance
- Enhanced Innovation and Creativity
- Greater Organizational Trust
- Career Advancement
- Personal Freedom and Relief

Challenges of Unhiding:

- Vulnerability
- Emotional Risk
- Potential for Misunderstanding
- Impact on Professional Image
- Retaliation Risk

Our differences make us unique and strong, pushing us to think outside the box. Education helps us understand our traumas and turn past pain into strength. As we unhide and embrace our true selves, we tap into these unique strengths that make us who we are. This journey is about recognizing and harnessing these qualities to foster genuine connections and personal growth.

Two Important Notes About Unhiding

- **Unhiding as a Privilege:** Recognize that unhiding is not always safe or possible for everyone. The ability to openly express personal aspects of yourself without fear of negative consequences is a privilege influenced by your environment. It is critical to consider steps two and three, finding people with whom you can safely share parts of yourself.

  Recognize that not everyone will be kind or accepting right away, we are still working toward a world of true inclusion and belonging.

- **The Impact of Culture and Beliefs:** Cultural background and personal beliefs shape how we show or hide parts of ourselves. They influence our archetypes and behaviors. Being aware of these influences helps us understand and accept ourselves and others better. Do the proactive work to understand and explore cultural expectations and norms; understanding these can reduce misunderstanding.

Reflection

We covered a lot in this section, including a framework for unhiding, strategies based on archetypes, and the impact of unhiding on Maslow's hierarchy of needs. Reflecting on your experiences can further support your journey of unhiding. Consider these questions to gain deeper insights:

1. **Personal Relationships:** Identify a personal relationship where hiding has played a role. How did these hiding behaviors create barriers or build trust? Write about a specific instance where revealing a hidden aspect changed the dynamic of the relationship. What emotions did you experience, and how did it affect your connection?

2. **Interpersonal Dynamics:** Describe a specific interaction where your archetype preference influenced your communication. How did you feel during and after the interaction? What emotions

did this situation bring up, and how did it impact your relationship with the other person?

3. **Community and Belonging**: Recall a time when you felt uncomfortable sharing personal information in a community setting. What fears or concerns influenced your decision to withhold or disclose? Consider how being more open in a supportive community could strengthen your sense of belonging and foster deeper connections. How could this change impact both you and the community?

Closing Insight: As you navigate the journey of unhiding, remember that it is both a personal and communal endeavor. The four-step framework of *Acknowledge*, *Invite*, *Build*, and *Share* provides practical steps to reveal your true self and foster deeper connections. By embracing these strategies, you not only pave the way for your own growth but also inspire others to begin their journeys of self-discovery.

Unhiding transforms environments into spaces where authenticity and inclusion thrive. It requires patience, empathy, and the courage to pause and allow others time to process your revelations. This journey is about creating a supportive community where everyone feels heard, valued, and understood.

Reflect on your own experiences of hiding and consider how they have shaped your interactions and self-perception. Use the tools and strategies discussed to take actionable steps toward a more authentic life.

TAKE THE FIRST STEP:
POSTCARD ACTIVITY

TAKE THE FIRST STEP

What are you hiding?
_____
_____
_____
_____

Gender & Age:
_____

Country:
_____

Participate in the Postcard Activity: The first step is acknowledge what you are hiding. Write down something about yourself that you've typically kept hidden. It could be a fear you've never spoken about, a dream you cherish, an aspect of your identity, or an opinion you've hesitated to express.

How It Works:

- **Scan to Start:** Access the anonymous postcard by using the QR code.

- **Write and Reflect:** Jot down your thoughts. This writing process helps bring your hidden aspects into the open.

Note: There is also a copy of the postcard at the very

end of the book that you can tear out and mail in for those who prefer hard copies.

Why Participate?

This exercise fosters introspection and marks a crucial step in moving toward fully embracing your authentic self. Writing down your hidden thoughts can be transformative—once you see your feelings and fears articulated, they become more real and harder to ignore, compelling you to address them. By participating, you're joining a community of voices, sharing and learning from the collective experience of hiding parts of ourselves.

Privacy and Sharing:

- **Private:** Keep your postcard for your personal reflection.
- **Anonymous Sharing:** Share your postcard anonymously in the Unhiding Community to help others learn from your experiences.
- **Trusted Sharing:** Share your postcard with someone you trust to open up opportunities for deeper connections and support.

It's About Taking the First Step.

NEXT STEPS

Now that you have a deeper understanding of personal unhiding and the strategies to support it, it's time to explore how these principles apply in the workplace. Let's delve into how unhiding can transform professional environments and encourage others to embrace their true selves.

CHAPTER 9

Strategies for Unhiding at Work

How can you unhide in the workplace? Unhiding allows you to bring your best self to work. This chapter offers strategies to foster a culture of openness in the workplace. Unhiding at work enhances collaboration, innovation, and overall performance, creating a more inclusive environment that supports diverse identities and promotes psychological safety.

With a cautious voice, the team member begins, "I need to take some time off next month."

When the supervisor asks if the vacation request could be postponed, the employee firmly responds, "That's not really an option for me."

"Why is it so urgent?" the supervisor presses gently.

After a pause, the employee admits softly, "I'm getting married."

The revelation catches the supervisor off guard. "I had no idea you were seeing someone. You've never mentioned anyone or brought anyone to our holiday parties. There aren't even photos on your desk."

With a deep breath, the employee unveils a hidden truth. "I know; I've been hesitant because I'm gay and wasn't sure how that would be received here."

The supervisor's demeanor instantly softens, understanding replacing surprise. "Thank you for sharing this with me and highlighting how isolated you've felt. I appreciate you bringing it to my attention."

The supervisor pauses.

"I understand how hard it can be to open up. A few years ago, I was hesitant to share about my personal life.

But I found when I did, my team was incredibly supportive. In this organization, we celebrate all life events here—big and small. How can we celebrate yours?"

Creating an inclusive workplace is a shared responsibility—it's a two-way street. Both leaders and employees play crucial roles, engaging in open communication and building trust. Leaders, in particular, need to model vulnerability, set a tone for openness, and create a psychologically safe environment for others to follow.

My advice: Leaders Go First.

When leaders take the first step, they act as a catalyst for change and connection. Moving away from old-school leadership styles that emphasize strict hierarchy and control, authentic leadership instead strengthens team bonds, improves customer relations, and enhances company culture. Sharing personal stories humanizes leaders, bridges gaps, and inspires employees. Celebrating different experiences and perspectives boosts creativity and innovation. This creates psychological safety and spaces where individuals can share their best selves, contributing to a more inclusive, creative, and successful workplace.

RESEARCH

Here is some more data: revealing your best self at work boosts belonging, engagement, and performance. Several studies, including those published in *Frontiers in Psychology*, the Harvard T.H. Chan School of Public Health, and *PLOS 1* support this. Leaders who inspire and connect with their team members create an environment that values authenticity, a key aspect of engaging leadership described by Wilmar B. Schaufeli in an article titled "Engaging Leadership: How to Promote Work Engagement?" in *Frontiers in Psychology* (2021). Transformational leadership significantly enhances engagement and trust, leading to more committed and aware employees (Harvard T.H. Chan School of Public Health, 2023). According to Schaufeli (2021), engaging leadership meets employees' needs for autonomy, competence, and connection, making work more engaging and effective.

Additionally, building authentic relationships at work reduces loneliness and improves health, job satisfaction, and productivity. Authenticity also improves performance, as employees who feel safe expressing themselves are more engaged, focused, and productive, findings supported by both Harvard's School of Public Health and Schaufeli's work.

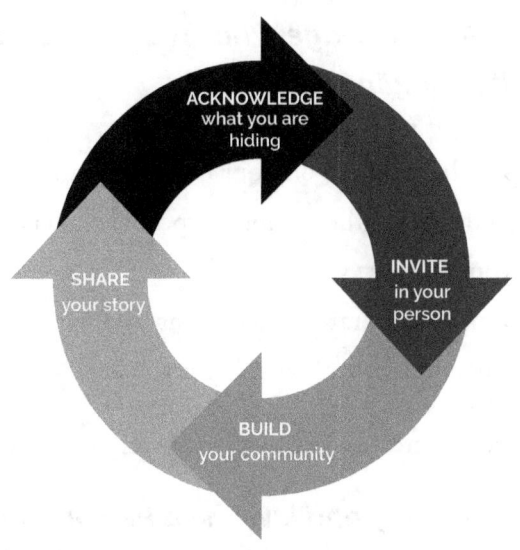

The four-step framework (introduced on page 80) not only helps you unhide in your personal life, it also fosters a supportive workplace environment. By acknowledging what you hide, inviting trusted individuals into your journey, building a community, and sharing your story, you create a culture of openness and connection. These steps, expanded upon here, are designed to guide you through the book, as well as your personal journey toward authenticity and connection. Let these steps empower you to be your best self and inspire others to do the same.

Step 1: Acknowledge What You Are Hiding and How It Is Holding You Back

1. **Leader:** Reflect on your own hidden aspects and understand the various types of hiders among your team.

2. **Employee:** Start by identifying what you are hiding and considering how it holds you back.

Pause and create space for introspection.

Step 2: Identify and Invite in a Person to Share Your Secret

- **Leader:** Begin with 'strategic unhiding' by sharing a personal challenge with your team to demonstrate the value of vulnerability.

- **Employee:** Share your story with a trusted colleague to foster self-acceptance and connection.

Pause and create space for questions.

Step 3: Build Your Community of Those with Shared Experiences

- **Leader:** Support and participate in diverse spaces that promote inclusivity and encourage employee resource groups—employee-led groups that provide support and networking opportunities.

- **Employee:** Connect with others who share similar experiences through online groups or workplace affinity and resource groups.

Pause and create space for questions.

Step 4: Share Your Story So Someone Else Can See Themselves in You

- **Leader:** Create opportunities to share your journey with your team through fireside chats, workshops, and team-building activities.
- **Employee:** Share your experiences in a small, trusted circle, such as employee resource groups, to foster empathy and a sense of belonging.

Pause and create space for questions.

Today's workplaces increasingly recognize the importance of creating an inclusive environment that celebrates belonging. Engaging leadership matters. Leaders play a crucial role in helping employees navigate self-awareness and trust-building, empowering everyone to unhide and thrive. Authentic and engaged leaders model and build deeper trust with their teams, creating a better and more psychologically safe work environment. Listening actively and recognizing others creates a culture where every voice is valued. When employees feel valued, loyalty, retention, and performance improve. By sharing their experiences, leaders show employees they are not alone, making talks more meaningful. Connections with customers and clients also improve when shared experiences matter.

Quick Considerations for Supporting Each Archetype:

- **The Guardian:** Offer support with sensitivity, respecting their need for privacy.
- **The Wonderer:** Foster openness through active listening and encouragement.
- **The Open Book:** Encourage depth while setting boundaries to ensure healthy sharing.
- **The Fortress:** Respect their pace and offer non-judgmental support.

Tools for Unhiding in the Workplace

- **Implement Rituals**: Offer regular check-ins, sharing circles, or workshops to encourage authentic interactions. Leaders should lead by example, sharing their own journeys and establishing structured feedback mechanisms to enhance transparency and trust.

- **Cultivate Safe Spaces:** Create settings where openness is encouraged and protected, and diverse perspectives and experiences are valued.

- **Acknowledge Courage:** Recognize and commend the bravery in yourself and others involved in unhiding, which can help ease the emotional challenges of sharing.

- **Promote Inclusivity:** Actively work to remove barriers that prevent safe unhiding, ensuring everyone can express their true selves without fear.

- **Demonstrate Leadership and Commitment:** The dedication of leaders to these efforts is vital. Leaders who actively support and prioritize their team's growth foster a culture of openness and authenticity. Effective communication about supportive programs encourages participation and commitment, creating an environment where everyone feels empowered to be their best selves.

By adopting these practices, workplaces can become more inclusive, supportive, and productive environments where everyone feels valued and understood.

A NOTE ABOUT NAVIGATING CHALLENGES WITH DIFFICULT MANAGERS

What if my manager is difficult?

Many of us have encountered a challenging manager. They might be disorganized, take credit for others' work, seem too busy, or communicate in unclear ways. These managers can be hard to approach, not very transparent, overly controlling, and hesitant to trust, which keeps people at a distance. They might micromanage, dismiss ideas, show favoritism, or be indecisive. Sound familiar?

If you struggle with a manager who discourages openness, try to maintain clear and professional communication, understand their perspective, build a supportive network of peers and mentors, proactively seek professional feedback, and demonstrate the benefits of openness and connection.

By starting with these strategies, you can create a more positive work environment for yourself and encourage a culture where people feel safe to unhide, share their true selves, and thrive. Even in the face of difficult management, your proactive efforts can lead to meaningful changes and a more fulfilling work experience.

While creating a better work environment for yourself, you may also be able to show your manager how to change their own behaviors, or quietly demonstrate to them the benefits of a different workplace approach.

<u>Note</u>: I didn't always get leadership right. By holding back and hiding, I missed opportunities for connection, creativity, and trust with my team. Over time, I learned that authentic leadership involves vulnerability and openness, which are essential for building strong relationships and increased performance.

Reflection

1. Reflect on a time at work when you unhid part of your identity or an opinion. What motivated this, and how did it impact your sense of belonging?

2. How does your workplace culture or community support or hinder unhiding? Are there practices or policies that encourage or obstruct openness?

3. Link your personal growth to professional interactions in terms of unhiding. How has becoming more authentic affected your professional relationships and your job?

4. Think of a leader you admire for their openness.

What traits do they show, and how do they affect their team's culture and effectiveness?

5. Reflect on a time you chose to hide or unhide at work. What influenced your decision, and what was the outcome?

6. How can you use the four-step framework to foster openness in your current role?

7. Envision an organizational change to promote unhiding. What steps are necessary, and what challenges might you face?

Closing Insight: The Liberating Power of Unhiding

Unhiding fosters connections that enhance both personal growth and workplace culture. By creating an environment of openness, you enrich your personal life and bolster professional innovation and engagement.

When people feel safe to be themselves, they become more engaged and motivated. Trust and open communication improve, leading to better teamwork. Innovation grows when diverse ideas are shared freely. Genuine connections among team members strengthen and enhance collaboration. Unhiding contributes to overall performance by creating a culture where everyone can thrive.

Although it requires managing vulnerabilities, the rewards of authenticity are immense and often outweigh the risks. This journey enhances both personal growth and community dynamics, leading to a more connected and fulfilling existence.

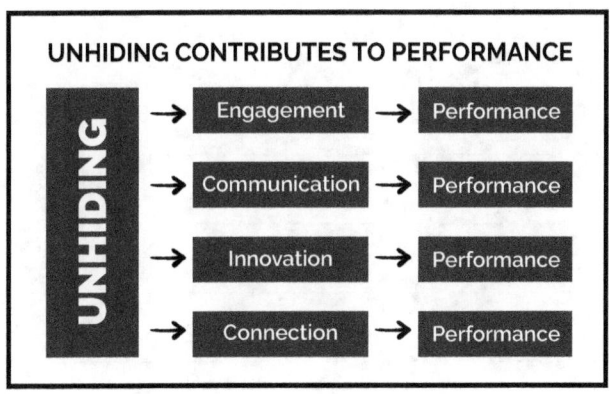

The graph illustrates the impact of unhiding on performance.

NOTES

CONCLUSION

The Journey Forward: Embracing Your Best Self

In this last section, we conclude with an empowering manifesto and a call to action. You'll be invited to join a community of individuals committed to unhiding and supporting each other on this path. By sharing your story and encouraging others to do the same, you contribute to a culture of connection and belonging.

CHAPTER 10

The Journey of Unhiding

Congratulations! As you reach the end of *Unhide &
Seek*, take a moment to reflect on the incredible journey
you have undertaken. Like all great heroes and heroines,
you have faced your fears, embraced your vulnerabilities,
and are transforming your life. You have entered a new
world, one where you are being true to yourself, and now
you are ready to live your life, feeling stronger and wiser.

Your journey doesn't end here. With the knowledge
and insights you have gained, you are now ready to be
your fullest and best self in every part of your life.

EMBRACE YOUR BEST SELF

As we have learned each archetype—The Guardian, The Wonderer, The Open Book, and The Fortress—offers unique lessons.

- **The Guardian:** Teaches you the value of being cautiously open to build trust and deeper connections.
- **The Wonderer:** Encourages curiosity and self-reflection, helping you understand yourself better and align with your core values.
- **The Open Book:** Shows the complexities of sharing too much and how to balance communication to attain true, healthy intimacy.
- **The Fortress:** Highlights the importance of slowly and selectively lowering your defenses to foster personal growth and enrich relationships.

Archetype	Key Lessons	Actionable Tips
The Guardian	Shows the value of cautious openness to build trust and deeper connections.	Set personal boundaries, share small secrets with trusted people, practice daily reflection.
The Wonderer	Encourages curiosity and self-reflection to understand oneself better.	Keep a curiosity journal, engage in active listening, join discussion groups, set personal development goals.
The Open Book	Highlights complexities of sharing too much and balancing communication.	Think before sharing, practice selective sharing, seek feedback on sharing habits, journal for clarity.
The Fortress	Shows the importance of lowering defenses gradually for personal growth and connection	Share small details first, schedule weekly check-ins, explore emotions through journaling, seek therapeutic support.

Here is a quick guide that captures the key lessons and strategies for unhiding.

Understanding the archetypes and their significance helps you build stronger connections, fostering a more inclusive, kind, and empathetic world.

The process of unhiding will continue as you live out your values, inspire others, and create spaces where everyone feels safe to be themselves. The wisdom you have gained is a powerful tool for change—use it to make the world more inclusive and vibrant.

Your Four-Step Journey of Unhiding

As you have been reading *Unhide & Seek*, you have already embarked on your own four-step process of unhiding.

- **Acknowledge:** By diving into these pages, you have acknowledged your desire to understand and reveal your true self.
- **Invite:** You invited me into your journey by engaging with the content and allowing my experiences and insights to resonate with you.
- **Build:** You have joined a community of like-minded individuals who are also on the path of unhiding, creating a support network.
- **Share:** You are now ready to share your story, using the tools and strategies you've learned, and connect with others through our shared website.

Unhiding isn't just about showing the world who you are; it's about aligning your life with what truly matters to you and living freely. Every step you take toward being more open boosts your personal growth and deepens your connections with others, setting the stage for a genuinely authentic life.

Remember, revealing your best self is a gradual process. Take it at your own pace, in your own way, and use what you've learned from this book to bring genuine authenticity and empathy into every relationship.

This journey isn't only about individual growth—it's about creating an environment of openness and authenticity that can revolutionize personal spaces and entire communities and workplaces. Keep pushing forward with bravery, curiosity, and the confidence to be unapologetically you. In the process, you might also help someone else unhide, too.

Create a personal commitment plan that outlines specific ways you will continue to unhide in your daily life. Regularly revisit and adjust this plan as you grow and learn more about yourself. Be kind to yourself and celebrate the steps you've taken to get to this point. Bravo!

FINAL REFLECTION EXERCISE: LETTER TO YOUR YOUNGER SELF

Think about the important moments in your life, those found on page 67. Write a letter to your younger self about these moments, offering insights and advice based on your journey of hiding and unhiding.

- Reflect on key moments where you felt the need to hide or chose to unhide.
- Write a letter offering advice and reassurances you needed at those times.
- Share your letter with someone you trust or in a group discussion open to conversations about shared experiences.

- Keep your letter as a way to look back as you continue your journey of unhiding and note your progress.

Link for Sharing: This last part of your journey involves sharing your story, encouraging others to unhide, and creating places where everyone feels accepted and valued.

Visit *Share Your Story* (https://ruthrathblott.com/share-your-story/) to continue sharing your journey and to connect with others on similar paths.

Thank you for trusting *Unhide & Seek* to guide you on this path. Remember, the journey of unhiding is ongoing, and each day presents new opportunities to live authentically and inspire others to do the same. Welcome to a life of greater freedom, focus, and fulfillment—centered on connection and the joy of building meaningful relationships—especially the one you have with yourself.

This may be the end of the book, but it's just the beginning of Unhiding and Seeking.

An Invitation to Join the Unhiding Movement

Unhiding Manifesto

Through Unhiding, I champion belonging by creating inclusive environments. I'm driven by a mission to embrace our uniqueness and address the fear of judgment that leads many to hide parts of themselves. It's time to connect authentically. I embrace acceptance, authenticity, and connection.

- *Celebrate Uniqueness:* I value human differences and celebrate our individuality.
- *Foster Inclusivity:* I work to build a culture where every voice is heard, valued, and respected, including those who have felt excluded from inclusion conversations.
- *Champion Equity:* I address inequalities to ensure equal opportunities for everyone, regardless of background, identity, or experience.
- *Create Safe Spaces:* I foster environments of trust and empathy where people feel safe and supported.
- *Embrace Connection:* I build meaningful connections through honesty and vulnerability.
- *Lead by Example:* I embody transparency, authenticity, and empathy as a leader in unhiding.
- *Amplify Voices:* I lift up underrepresented and marginalized voices, recognizing their invaluable contributions, while ensuring that no one feels excluded from the conversation.
- *Develop a Humanity Practice:* I nurture compassion, empathy, and kindness, fostering a practice of humanity in my daily interactions and decisions.
- *Promote Personal Growth:* I provide resources for personal and professional growth within a nurturing environment.
- *Unleash Potential:* I create safe spaces that empower individuals to realize their full potential and foster innovation.
- *Drive Change:* I persistently push boundaries to strive for a more inclusive world.

Unhiding is a movement. I strive to transform how individuals perceive themselves and others, ultimately creating a world where people can unhide, thrive, and belong.

_____   _____
SIGNATURE   DATE

LET'S CONTINUE THE CONVERSATION

Hey, it's Ruth!

Thank you for joining me on the journey through *Unhide & Seek*.

I see you.

I hope that no matter where you find yourself on your personal journey, you've discovered something transformative within these pages. Your courage and boldness in embarking on this journey are truly amazing. You are part of a growing movement toward transparency and supporting others in their quest to unhide. To make a significant impact, we need to work together and encourage each other.

Here's how you can get involved in the Unhiding Movement and help it grow:

Share a quick review.

Your opinion matters. If you are like me, you value other people's recommendations when looking for a good book, especially one that challenges our mindset and creates conversation. Please go to the website where you purchased this book, search for "Ruth Rathblott" and "*Unhide and Seek*," and leave a review. It's the greatest gift you could give me and it helps to share this idea with others. Thank you!

Share it on social.

Take a selfie with the book.

Send it to: ruth@ruthrathblott.com and share it on social media. Add at the end: #UnhideAndSeek

Gift this book.

If *Unhide & Seek* resonated with you and you know someone who would benefit from it, consider gifting a copy. It's a thoughtful gesture for friends, colleagues, or family members and a great choice for book clubs, retreats, and workshops.

For bulk orders of 10 or more, I can help you secure significant savings. This is ideal for training, events, and spreading Ruth Rathblott's insights on embracing uniqueness and fostering inclusion. We can even customize the books with a note from the CEO and include a custom video message from me. Please email ruth@ruthrathblott.com to set up a time to connect.

Invite me to speak to your organization.

I'm available for a limited number of speaking and consulting engagements. If you'd like to bring the powerful message of *Unhide & Seek* to your workplace, please contact: ruth@ruthrathblott.com or visit ruthrathblott.com.

Now that you understand yourself better, you can help someone else do the same.

Join this global movement of unhiding!

Resources for Continued Growth

Visit *RuthRathblott.com*

Unhiding our differences is not a weakness; it is a strength. It is the courage to be myself, fully and unapologetically.

Learn about the powerful effects of revealing your true self and how embracing vulnerability can strengthen personal relationships and improve your professional life. Explore the transformative power of unhiding: deepened personal connections and enhanced professional dynamics. Understand the privileges, benefits, and challenges of being open and how it can affect your life in many ways.

GRATITUDE

If you want to go fast, go alone.
If you want to go far, go together.
—African proverb

Editorial Board

A heartfelt thank you to my incredible editorial board–Art Chang, Cathy Fyock, Julie Sanders Keymer, Joleen Lawson, Mark LeBlanc, Braxton Midyette, and Stuart Rossen—and the meticulous editing from Elizabeth Arterberry and Christine Borris. Your wisdom, insight, and dedication have been instrumental in shaping this book.

Special Thanks

Gratitude to Carol Argento, Yvonne Buysman, Jennifer Byrne, Wendy Anderson Cocke, Denise Gabel, Phillip and Suzanne Handal, Marc Johnson, Larry Leister, Chris Maher, Jeff Martinka, Nell Merlino, Paul Rathblott, Maria Rosati, Kerry Ryan, Carol Saline, April Salomon, Dena Warren, The Lucky Fin Project family, and my abundant-mindset NSA-NYC community. Your unwavering support, encouragement, and belief in this project have been invaluable. Each of you has played a unique role in helping me bring this vision to life.

The Universe, I trust you completely.

Readers and Supporters

To all the wonderful people who reached out after reading *Singlehandedly*, and to the courageous individuals who have shared their hiding and unhiding journeys after hearing me speak, thank you. Your stories about how the book impacted your lives and your words of encouragement have meant the world to me. You inspired me to keep going, and your feedback has fueled my passion for this work. Knowing that my words have touched your lives is the greatest reward.

Your bravery in opening up and sharing your stories has been profoundly moving and inspiring. Your willingness to be vulnerable is a testament to your strength and has deeply enriched my understanding of the human experience. Your stories remind us all of the power of connection and the importance of being seen and heard. Keep unhiding!

Together We Thrive

I wrote this book with a clear purpose: to help anyone who is hiding come out into the light. I hope *Unhide & Seek* provides the insights and tools from my own experiences and the stories shared by others to empower you to embrace your best self sooner. If even one person can break free from the constraints of hiding and find genuine connection and fulfillment, then this journey has been worthwhile.

This book is a testament to the power of community and collaboration. It is a reminder that we are stronger together, and that we can achieve great things by supporting one another. Thank you to everyone who has been a part of this journey. Your contributions, big and small, have made all the difference.

With deepest gratitude and warmest wishes,

Ruth

P.S.
AUTHOR REFLECTION

I Have Been All Four

In my journey of self-discovery and acceptance, I have experienced being The Guardian, The Wonderer, The Open Book, and The Fortress. Understanding each archetype has helped me grow and taught me important lessons about being vulnerable, honest, and connecting with others.

The Guardian: Rituals of Hiding

For many years, I hid my limb difference like The Guardian would. I wore certain clothes, positioned my body in specific ways, and chose topics that kept attention away from my hand. I thought this would protect me from judgment or rejection. I explore this more in my first book, *Singlehandedly: Learning to Unhide and Embrace Connection.*

The Wonderer: Curiosity and Journals and People

Even while hiding, I was curious about myself. I kept journals and went to therapy, trying to understand what I was hiding and how to stop. My disability, once a source of insecurity, became a strength, shaping my personal and professional lives. My greatest vulnerability turned into one of my most powerful assets.

The Open Book: Strategic Sharing

As I grew more comfortable with my disability, I started to share my story. Like The Open Book, I became more open but kept some things private to build strong relationships while maintaining control over what I shared.

The Fortress: Boundaries and Protection

Sometimes, I needed to be like The Fortress, setting strong boundaries to protect myself and others. I had to decide when to share and when to keep things private for safety.

Integrating the Archetypes

Living as these different types has been a balance of hiding and sharing. Each phase taught me more about myself and how I relate to others. The Guardian taught me about the fears that kept me silent. The Wonderer encouraged self-reflection. The Open Book showed me the complexity of connections and sharing. The Fortress emphasized setting boundaries and when to hold back for psychological safety.

I learned that our identities are made up of many parts influenced by cultural, social, and personal factors. Embracing our different identities means recognizing the diverse backgrounds and perspectives we bring. Things like race, gender, sexuality, and money shape our experiences of hiding and unhiding.

Creating safe environments where everyone feels free to be their best self is essential. This means listening to others' experiences, promoting empathy, and supporting diversity and inclusion. By understanding and accepting our full identities, we can build stronger connections and a more caring world.

As I continue this journey, I am committed to promoting inclusivity and intersectionality. Embracing our unique identities and creating spaces where everyone feels valued helps unlock our true potential and that of our communities.

Closing Insight: All the Faces of Ruth

I embody all four archetypes and am continually working on understanding my hiding behaviors and choices to unhide.

This journey is not about choosing one archetype but understanding how each one appears in our lives and affects our interactions. Embrace this journey with curiosity, courage, and an open heart. See how it transforms your interactions and helps you be more authentic and connected.

Let this guide you to a fuller understanding of who you are and who you can become. Connect to your possibilities.

MEET THE AUTHOR

Inspirational speaker Ruth Rathblott, MSW, is a TEDx speaker, the international bestselling author of *Singlehandedly: Learning to Unhide and Embrace Connection*, and an award-winning former CEO of a nonprofit organization. Through her work as a consultant and coach, she has worked in both corporate and educational settings, and she has staged podcasts, webinars, and  "fireside chats." Ruth has been instrumental in transforming workplace cultures, and she is dedicated to fostering inclusion, providing opportunities for those who face obstacles, and promoting a more connected world.

Born with a limb difference, Ruth speaks passionately on issues of inclusion, belonging, and the empowerment that comes from embracing one's unique attributes. Her advocacy focuses on transforming perspectives and encouraging individuals to accept and celebrate their unique differences as strengths.

Ruth's professional journey includes leading roles at Big Brothers Big Sisters of New York City and the Harlem Educational Activities Fund, where she championed youth mentoring through education and community engagement. In 2014, Ruth was given the Smart CEO Brava! Award and profiled as a CEO in *The New York Times'* Corner Office, which featured her passion and motivation for leadership. Ruth received the Trailblazer Award from the Community Resource Exchange in 2019 and the Unsung Hero Award from the Female Founders Alliance in 2020. In 2023, she received the Gedaliah Award from the National Speakers' Association of NYC.

Ruth resides in New York City. She serves on the boards of The Lucky Fin Project, supporting individuals with limb differences, and her alma mater, Goucher College. You can learn more about Ruth, her work, and the Unhiding Movement at ruthrathblott.com.

Read Ruth's bestselling first book,

Singlehandedly
Learning to Unhide and Embrace Connection

What are you hiding?

Chances are there is something about you that makes you different, that makes you feel you don't belong. Many of us hide our ethnicity, sexuality, mental health, disability, religion... the list goes on. The diversity and inclusion movement has emboldened some to come out of the shadows. But too often disability is not included in that conversation.

Ruth Rathblott was born with a limb difference. In her compelling and intimate memoir, she counts the exhausting and often lonely years she spent overachieving and trying to hide her disability before she learned to unhide. She takes us on a journey of self-discovery: discovering her difference, being taught to hide it, and ultimately finding self-acceptance and connection with others.

This book will show you how to build a world of true acceptance, inclusion, and belonging. By the end, you will understand the need to:

- Own your difference—it's your greatest gift!
- Find connection and community by allowing others in to support you
- Create inclusive conversations that allow for curiosity and empathy
- Recognize why representation is essential to creating an inclusive environment
- Realize the power of sharing your story

Singlehandedly is a book for all of us who have been hiding our differences and want to find freedom, for leaders who want to build more inclusive teams, and for diversity and inclusion directors committed to expanding the diversity conversation to include everyone.

Connect with Ruth

www.RuthRathblott.com

LinkedIn: ruth-rathblott

Instagram: ruthrath

Youtube: @ruthrathblott62

Join Ruth's free email monthly UNHIDING newsletter
and get regular inspiration, tips, lessons,
and encouragement.

https://ruthrathblott.com/contact/

TAKE THE FIRST STEP

We invite you to participate in this powerful activity by sharing what you are hiding. Simply follow these steps:

1. **Fill Out the Postcard:** Take a moment to reflect and write down what you are hiding on the lines provided. Include your gender, age, and country.
2. **Rip Out the Postcard:** Carefully tear along the edge to remove this postcard from the book.
3. **Mail It In:** Attach a stamp in the designated spot and mail your completed postcard to:

UNHIDE & SEEK
PO BOX 230054
New York, NY 10023 USA

By sharing your story, you are taking the first step toward unhiding and connecting deeply. We look forward to hearing from you!

TAKE THE FIRST STEP

What are you hiding?

_____

_____

_____

_____

Gender & Age: _____

Country: _____

UNHIDE & SEEK
PO BOX 230054
New York, NY 10023

USA